CANAJAN, EH?

CANAJAN, EH?

Text by Mark M. Orkin

Illustrations by Bickerstaff

Third Revised Edition

Copyright © 1997, 1988, 1982, 1973
by Mark M. Orkin
Illustrations © 1997, 1988 by Don Evans

Published in 1997 by
Stoddart Publishing Co. Limited
34 Lesmill Road
Toronto, Canada
M3B 2T6

First edition published in 1973
Revised editions published in 1982, 1988

Distributed in Canada by
General Distribution Services Limited
34 Lesmill Road, Toronto, Canada M3B 2T6
Tel. (416) 445-3333
Fax (416) 445-5967
Email Customer.Service@ccmailgw.genpub.com

Distributed in the U.S. by
General Distribution Services Inc.
85 River Rock Drive, Suite 202,
Buffalo, New York 14207
Toll-free tel. 1-800-805-1083
Toll-free fax 1-800-481-6207
Email gdsinc@genpub.com

01 00 99 98 97 1 2 3 4 5

Cataloging in Publication Data

Orkin, Mark M., 1917–   .
    Canajan eh?

3rd revised edition

ISBN 0-7737-5906-9

1. English language – Canada – Humor.
2. Canadianisms (English) – Humor.*
I. Bickerstaff, Isaac.   II. Title.

PN6178.C30735 1997   427'.971'0207
97-931962-5

Cover design: Pekoe Jones
Cover illustration: Bickerstaff
Design and typesetting: Kinetics Design & Illustration

Printed in Canada

*We gratefully acknowledge the Canada Council for the
Arts and the Ontario Arts Council for their support of
our publishing program.*

**TO MY FATHER
AND MOTHER
WHO DISCOVERED
CANADA**

Let us get nearer to the fire, so that
we can see what we are saying.
The Bubis of Fernando Po

PREFACE

In the years since this little work first saw the light of day, the Canajanization of our country has proceeded apace, or rather ameter (*see* Metrickery).

Since Canajan came out of the closet, more people have been speaking it than ever before. Indeed, one province felt obliged to pass a law prohibiting its use. To no avail. Canajan, like the Sen Lornz River, just keeps rolling along.

As appears from the pages that follow, some old familiar faces have gone while others seem to be with us forever (*see* Plitticul Signs): the ecology is big (*see* Half Acid Rain); eye denty is small but growing (*see* Canajan Content); culture is all over the landscape (*see* Litter Choor); and the Moundies, although still riding musically, are now marching to a different drummer (*see* Arsey Em Pee).

Being concerned merely to record what has been happening around us, we withhold editorial comment. It is for others to judge whether those changes are good or bad. Enough for our purposes to note that as the world slouches toward the year 2000 Canajans find themselves, as never before, united in the strife that divides them, still speaking Canajan, and greatly relieved at the prospect that the Twenty-first Century, when it finally arrives, will belong to someone else.

INTRODUCTION

Since it is a bilingual country Canada has four languages. This gives fullest scope to linguistic self-expression while considerably increasing the likelihood of misunderstanding.

It is customary to divide the Canajan population into *Francophone* and *Anglophone*.* On the French Canajan side the fishle language is French, used for statutes, classics, scholarly journals, and the things that nobody bothers to read. Most French Canajans, while they read and write French, talk Joual, the nash null language of Quebec. It is not necessary to teach Joual since every native son and daughter already speaks it. Besides, no manuals of instruction exist. Why should they?

On the English Canajan side the fishle language is

*These terms are thought by some to derive from two early communications systems, one operated mainly in Quebec by la Mère Cloche and the other in English-speaking parts of the country by Ma Bell. As parallel groups of subscribers cohered around their respective party lines, the division of Canajans into two main linguistic communities developed into the social and political reality which we know today. The subsequent merger of the two telephone systems (whose head office was symbolically located in the Province of Quebec) occurred too late to materially affect the linguistic division of the country.

English, the language of parliamentary debates, Royal Commission reports, book reviews, and all the speeches that no one bothers to listen to. Most English Canajans, though they are able to write English, talk Canajan, the nash null language of English Canada. As with Joual, no formal instruction in Canajan is either given or necessary. Who would need it? All Anglos speak Canajan from birth.

Some years ago a self-styled professor at the University of Sinney compiled a lexicon of Strine, the nash null language of Australia. I had hoped that his opposite number at the University of Tronna (*see* You've Tea) would accept the challenge and produce a study of Canajan, but this was to overestimate our academics' concern for Canajan content. Although the University of Tronna has long been known as the hotbed of Canajan (along with the University of Albirda at Kail Gree, and Eubie Sea) the language of instruction and research in these places has always been English. Canajan was and is consistently downgraded, ridiculed, or ignored by our scholars.

In part this happened because Canajan academics have been far too busy suppressing (or supporting) demonstraders, and attacking (or defending) the nomination of Mare Cans to faculty appointments to devote much time to Canajan studies. They also feared that to call attention to the existence of Canajan might leave the impression the Anglos were illiterate — much as educated Quebeckers pretended until recently that Joual did not exist, while busily trying to wash it out of their children's mouths with soap and water. But fortunately such backward attitudes are passing away in both cultures, and with the growing Mare Canzation of our campuses we may look to see Canajan Studies (along with Joual Studies) accorded their rightful place in academic curricula. To help remedy this default the brief glossary of Canajan which follows has been compiled.

It may come as a surprise to discover that the main characteristics of Canajan are identical with those of Joual. For it is a fact that the two nash null languages of Canada display precisely the same qualities. These will emerge in the pages which follow, but for convenience they may briefly be listed as: a nimiety of neologisms, an impudicity of pronunciation, a crapulence of grammar, a prurience of syntax, and a necrosis of Mare Canisms.

No standard of Canajan has yet been established. Hence domestic readers may encounter some expressions here and there with which they are unfamiliar, but all specimens have been carefully gathered in the field. On the other hand, forners need exercise no caution in using this text since all terms discussed will be understandable by somebody somewhere in Canada. And all are, beyond question, Canajan.

A

ABOOT Canajan adverb and preposition of place.
As in: 'Wearya bin?' 'Oot and aboot.'
See Oot.

ACRID Careful and precise.
As in: 'The Minster of
Fie Nance has an acrid mind.'

ACCURST What happens in or to one's mind.
As in: 'It accurst to me.'

AERO Pointed missile launched from a bow.
As in:
I shotten aero inta tha yair,
It felta earth I noona 'twere.
Also: the Youstin Aeros.

AGGER CULCHER	The art of cultivating the soil. As in: 'Leamie innerjuice the Minster of Agger Culcher.'
AIR	To make mistakes. As in the Canajan proverb: 'To air is yoomin, toofer give duhvine.' Also the nominal use. As in: 'No hits, no runs, no airs.'
ALBIRDA	Non-dues-playing member of OPEC, reaper of royalties, champion of the overdog, everybody's rich uncle, time was when Albirda had it made.

Only yesterday, when Albirda's assets were all tied up in cash, people forgot how for years and years tough times made insomnia of the Western Dream. In those days Albirda fared poorly, with only the Schnook wind to keep her warm. By contrast, Beesee had rockier mountains, Skatchwan wavier grain, Mantoba brawnier sons, Untario niagrier falls, Kwee Beck fairer daughters, and so on. At a time when other provinces seemed abrim with nature's goodies, Albirdans didn't have a potash to peon.

Well, things are always darkest just before the dawn, as they say, and early one morning it dawned on some oil-producing countries that the only difference between dollar-a-barrel oil and forty-dollar-a-barrel oil is *chutzpa*. With that OPEC was off and gouging, and before you could say cartel Albirda had opted for the

17

old desert principle: never give the buyer a fair sheikh. It proved to be a shrewd decision.

Several years and some billions of dollars later Albirdans were riding tall in the saddle when all at once the bottom fell out of the oil barrel and Albirdans fell off their horse. Worse was to come when Wayne Gretzky, the province's other natchurl resource, went the way of oil prices and lost first place to Mario Le Mew, a high-scoring cat among the penguins. Even worse was to come when they traded Number 99 to the L.A. Kings for $15 mil., which used to be small change in the old days. Now people on the streets of Kailgree and Emmuntun are asking each other: 'Is it out of the oil patch and back to the cabbage patch?' Once again Albirdans were in step with the rest of the country.

ANGLO   A non-French Canajan Canajan.

ANGLODESH   The homeland of Quebec's English-speaking population when and if the province subdivides.

Once Canajans learned to think the unthinkable about the possibility of Quebec's leaving (*see* Sepper Tizzum), it became clear to some people that the only solution to the problem of two nations warring within the bosom of a single province was the Solomonic one.

In Montreal the civic leaders of Westmount, having

already held their own referendum, were now debating what to call the new territories. Councillor Ecks moved that the two subdivisions of the old province be named East Quebec and West Quebec, modelled after East Pakistan and West Pakistan. Motion lost: too Asian. Councillor Wye proposed North Quebec and South Quebec, like the Carolinas or the Dakotas. Motion lost: too American. Councillor Zed offered Upper Quebec and Lower Quebec, patterned on the old pre-Confederation model. Motion lost: after only a few years Anglos were already tired of being on the bottom.

When he got wind of the debate, presidential candidate Lucien Bouchard, speaking for the Rest of Quebec (*see* ROQ), told a hastily organized rally at Ben's Delicatessen in downtown Montreal that his people (*see* Poor Len) had held the patent on the name Quebec since way before 1759. That was the year when the Brits snuck in like a Wolfe in the night and took Abraham's plains away from him while New France slept. 'Who steals my purse steals trash,' Mr. Bouchard thundered (referring to the depressed state of the Quebec economy because of Ottawa's failure to hand out enough money), 'but he that filches from me my good name makes me poor indeed!' When a woman in the audience pointed out that Mr. Bouchard was quoting from Shakespeare, he replied with some heat that Corneille had been the first to use something like those words, adding, 'and the Anglos stole them from us the way they stole everything else, but just wait: we intend to make them pay for it *PAR LE NEZ!!!'* *

After a debate lasting late into the night, the Westmount council voted unanimously to name their new territory *Anglodesh* in recognition of Canada's multiculturalism. The name had the added advantage of reading the same in both English and French, so no need for bilingual signs at the frontier. It should not take too long to figure out where to locate the frontier either, because Anglos have always known where to draw the line, eh?

Meantime, Mr. Bouchard has rented the old Montreal Forum on Atwater Street as the venue for delivering his official response to the Westmount initiative. According to a late-breaking story on *The National*, as a goodwill gesture the Westmount councillors have offered to waive Angledeshi visas on a one-time basis for all valid ticket-holders.

In an e-mail letter to the editor of The Gazette, *Aleister MacFarlane, chairman of the French department at McGill, pointed out that the Standard French for 'to make someone pay through the nose' is not* payer par le nez *but rather* tenir la dragée haute à quelq'un, *to which a spokesman for l'Office de la Langue Française replied: 'Qu'sait-i'? C't'un maudzit anglo!'*

ANTABOTICKS

Stuff that kills bacteria.

AP ZURD

Ridiculous, preposterous. As in: 'It's jiss ap zurd, Linda, ta sear withim.'

ARDIC

The far north, home of the In You Wit, one of Canada's two found-in races, *q.v.* Of or pertaining to northern areas, boreal.

The Ardic, as one of the world's leading producers of snow, benefitted for many years from a high world demand for this commodity which reached its peak during the gold rush of '98. The market later became depressed during World War I, although it picked up again when the skiing craze swept Canada in the twendies and thirdies.

World War II caused demand for the natural product to decline sharply. As a result the Ardic was left with vast stocks and no markets other than the Knighted States which was not slow in proposing a con nendal snow paul see to help sustain the Cold War.

Many Canajans felt that it was morally wrong to use a strategic material like snow for aggressive purposes and demonstaders quickly appeared outside Hugh Ess diplomatic offices in many cities. Others opposed the Ardic becoming a branch plant of the Mare Can snow industry and more demostraders paraded on Parl Meant

Hill at Oddawa in sub-zero weather. In addition letters were written to newspaper editors, and the Seabee See did a half-hour television show on trapping Ardic foxes.

Always responsive to public opinion, the guv munt tried to dispose of their stockpiles of snow in Yourp, but this was blocked by anti-dumping measures imposed by the E.U. Some effort was then made to expand the domestic market under the Regional Disparity Program, but this would have involved a costly structure of price supports which failed to gain opposition approval in the Cent, the guv munt as usual being in a minority position.

The whole scheme finally came to grief at the next Fed Rull Per Vinshull Conference when Kwee Beck announced that snow came under per vinshull jurisdiction by reason of the property and civil rights sub-section of the Beanay Act, *q.v.* The conference broke up when Kwee Beck's spokesman stated that they would never permit the wholesale importation of low-cost Ardic snow into the province thereby reducing the number of snow jobs normally available as part of their winter works program.

An awful lot of snow blew away along with the old Soviet Union, and with the thawing of the Cold War the fragile economy of the Ardic collapsed. There were fewer igloo starts that year than in any previous twelve-month period, and Employment Insurance was extended to all In You Wit, whether they were looking for work or not, thereby putting them on an equal footing with the rest of the country.

ARM SEE   Royal Military College at Kingsten, Untario.

ARSEY EM PEE   Founded by Sir John, Eh? in 1873, for almost a hundred years the Moundies enjoyed great P.R. They always got their man, they rode musically, and they sang like Nelson Eddy. They also could do no wrong, as witness their motto "Maintiens le droit" (I maintain we're right).

Their story read like one triumph after another: they helped catch and hang Louis Riel; a squadron was sent to Siberia after the revolution to help put down the Bolshies; it returned home the following year in time to help break the Winnipeg General Strike. They were our first line of defence against Comma Nizzum (*q.v.*), as witness their motto "Maintiens le droit" (Keep to the right).

But in time rumours spread that the Moundies had descended from those lofty ideals in order to open people's junk mail, and were spending more and more time in the bedrooms of the nation (*see* Paul Ticks). When people asked what they were doing in the bedroom the Solicitor General answered that they were merely seeing that the machinery of state was kept in good order, as witness their motto "Maintiens le droit" (Maintenance is our right). By definition, he pointed out, undercover activities have to be performed under the covers. This satisfied nobody.

Finally, the MacDonald Royal Commission established that what the Moundies had been up to in the bedrooms of the nation was dirty tricks. That meant an awful lot of linen had to be sent to the laundry, after which the Moundies rode off into the sunset singing to the MacDonald Commission: "We did it all for you." As the last barn burned to the ground Canajans loved them more than ever.

Next thing that happened was the lovely people who brought you Disneyworld took over marketing and turned the once-proud force into a Mickey Mouse operation.

ASBESTOS

To the extent of your ability. As in: 'You'll haveta make do asbestos you can.'

ASSESSIBLE

Able to be reached. As in: 'The town of Shawvl (*q.v.*) is easily assessible by road from Oddawa.' The nominal form, assessibility, is less common.

ASSESSORIES

Things that go with other things. As in: 'Howja like mnoo dress, Linda?' 'Grade, Susan, an scott matchin assessories too.'

BANCA CANDA | The mat upon which bad things get wrestled to the ground. *See* Deaf Sit.

BAWLCONY | Verandah with access from upper storey of dwelling house or apartment building; gallery in a theatre.

BEANAY ACT | Briddish statute of 1867 providing for the union of Untario, Kwee Beck, Nove Skoshuh, and Noob Runzwig. The other provinces came in later at reduced rates. *See* Sir John, Eh?

BEAT OUT | To overcome, vanquish, clobber. As in: 'The Leafs beat out Deetroyit for lass place in the Westren Con-fronts.'

BEERACRAT | Guv munt functionary who eats, drinks, and grows fat at taxpayers' expense.

BEESEE	The most westren Canajan province.
BEIG	A container made of paper, cloth, etc., with opening at top. Rhymes with German *Feig*. Oddawa Valley Canajan.
BEINCK	A building where Canajans keep their money. The traveller who pauses at a crossroads in the Oddawa Valley and sees on the four corners a beer-hall, a Catholic church, a grocery store, and a beinck, knows that he has at last reached the Canajan heartland.
BELIAL, STRAIT OF	An arm of the Atlantic Ocean lying between the coasts of Labberdor and Noophun Lund. Forms the northern outlet of the Gulfa Sen Lornz.
BERREX	Buildings where soldiers are lodged.
BERRIE	Town in Untario about fifty miles north of Tronna.

BERRIERS	Things that get in the way of other things. As in: 'First yagodda liminade innerpervinshuĺ terrif berriers.'
BERRIL	A cylindrical vessel made of hooped wooden staves.
BIDDER	Not sweet.
BLEEDING	Crying like a calf.
BLING YULE	Adjective applied to an English Canajan who has been obliged to learn French to make a living.
BLOOJ, EHS?	Tronna's response to the Mare Can League, based on the premise that if the Japanese can play *basuboru* the Canajans could hardly do worse. After winning the World Series in 1992-93 on the strength of their legendary spitball, the Blooj, Ehs? have struck out ever since, exemplifying the received wisdom that if it's Canajan it can't be any good.
BODAYDO	A plant with farinaceous tubers used as food.
BODDUM	The lowest part; the backside. Used as a toast: 'Boddum Zup!'
BOG SITE	Stuff they use to make loomanumb, *q.v.*

BOMB LINE — Place where the company whose hot stock you bought last year admits how much money it lost this year. Also metaphorically, as in: 'C'mon, c'mon, gimme tha bomb line.'

BRIDDISH — Of or pertaining to Grade Bridden. Sometimes contracted to Brish, as in: Brish Commwealth.

BRIDDI SHYLES — England, Scotland, Wales, and Northern Ireland. Commonly called the You Kay.

BRISH CLUMBYA — *See* Beesee.

BROODLE Savage, cruel. As in: 'I tellya, Rick, the Leafs' lass game was sumpm broodle.'

BUDDER Yellow, fatty substance produced by churning cream. As in: 'Id tace bedder with budder.' May be used figuratively. As in: 'Doan budder me yup.'

BUGGETT A wood metal pail for carrying water. *See* Torrance.

BUSTA A transportation term. As in: 'Wenza busta Swiff Kernt?' 'Quorda too.' 'Thang slot.'

BYNOW *See* Harya.

CABBIDAL

The siddy where the seat of plitti cull power is locaded. As in: 'Kwee Beck Siddy is the per vinshull cabbidal.' Also refers to accumulated wealth. As in: Cabbidal gains tacks.

CAB NET

The executive committee of Minsters which, under the Prime Inster, directs state paul see. *See* Paul Ticks.

CAIRP

Small town locaded on the Cairp River west of Oddawa.

CANA DUT

A person running for public office who tries to bribe you with your own money to vote for him. As in: 'Heeza cana dut in the necks mewni sippul (fed rull, per vinshull, etc.) lexshun.'

CANAJAN

Four meanings are commonly distinguished.
1. Of Canada or its inhabitants.
2. A person of Canajan birth or nationality.
3. An Anglo, *q.v.*
4. The nash null language of Anglos.

CANAJAN CONTENT

The only thing that distinguishes Canajan from Mare Can television.

For years the See Arty See, *q.v.*, sought to purge this notoriously insalubrious medium and render it fit for the more sensitive Canajan ears, eyes, nose, and throat.

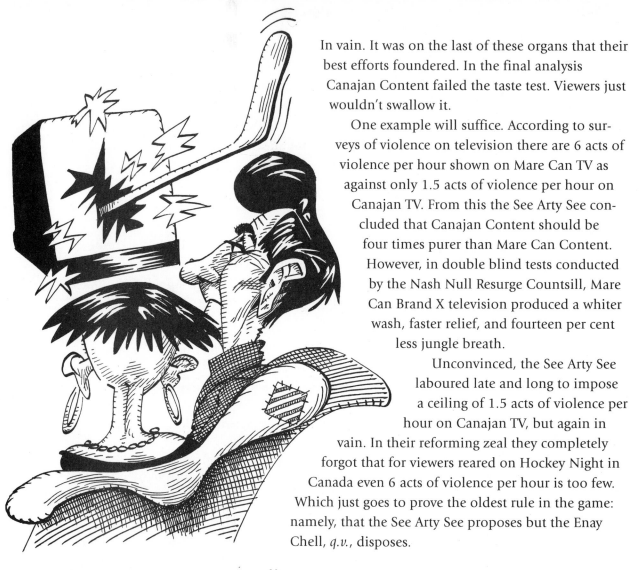

In vain. It was on the last of these organs that their best efforts foundered. In the final analysis Canajan Content failed the taste test. Viewers just wouldn't swallow it.

One example will suffice. According to surveys of violence on television there are 6 acts of violence per hour shown on Mare Can TV as against only 1.5 acts of violence per hour on Canajan TV. From this the See Arty See concluded that Canajan Content should be four times purer than Mare Can Content. However, in double blind tests conducted by the Nash Null Resurge Countsill, Mare Can Brand X television produced a whiter wash, faster relief, and fourteen per cent less jungle breath.

Unconvinced, the See Arty See laboured late and long to impose a ceiling of 1.5 acts of violence per hour on Canajan TV, but again in vain. In their reforming zeal they completely forgot that for viewers reared on Hockey Night in Canada even 6 acts of violence per hour is too few. Which just goes to prove the oldest rule in the game: namely, that the See Arty See proposes but the Enay Chell, *q.v.*, disposes.

CANAJAN LEEJUN | A vedderans' organization dedicated to refighting past wars.

CANDA The attributive form of Canada, the nation-state of all Canajans. As in Canda Countsil; Stastistics Canda; Canda Dry, etc.

CANE Variant of 'Canajan.' As in: Cane Tire, Cane Psiffic, etc.

CENT The appointive branch of parl meant. *See* Paul Ticks.

CENTRES Members of the Cent, *q.v.*

CHAIR TEA Eleemosynary instooshn. As in: 'A danation ta the chair tea of yer choice wud be appreshated.'

CHEWSDY The day after Mundy. *See* Sundy.

CHOOB Hollow cylinder; also component part of a radio or TV set. *See* Toob.

CLAIRFY To make a statement or idea intelligible. As in: 'Hope flea icon clairify that for you.'

CLIMB IT Canada has four kinds of weather — hot, cold, wet, and snowy. Hence the only permitted conversational gambits relating to climb it are: 'Hottanuff furya?', 'Coldanuff furya?', 'Wetanuff furya?', and 'Snowyanuff furya?' These may be abbreviated to: 'Hot, eh?', 'Cold,

eh?', 'Wet, eh?', and 'Snowy, eh?' It would be meaningless and also unidiomatic to ask anyone: 'Nice anuff
furya?' No such expression exists in Canajan.

COLUMN | Quiet or tranquil. *See* Kam.

COMMA NIZZUM | System of social organization, particularly as developed
by Marks and Lennon. The opposite of Free Dumb, *q.v.*

CON NENDEL | Anything for the benefit of the Mare Cans. As in:
'Washton calls for a Con Nendel Wadder Paul See.'

CONSTOOSHN | The system of laws and conventions by which Canada
tries and sometimes almost succeeds in governing
herself. Many countries have noble or inspiring con-
stooshnl aims like 'Life, Liberty, and the Pursuit of
Happiness' or 'Liberty, Equality, Fraternity.' By contrast,
the aims of the Canajan constooshn are defined in sec-
tion 91 of the Brish North America Act as 'Peace, Order,
Good Government, and Boredom.' *See* Beanay Act.

COUNTSIL | Administrative body of municipality. As in: Siddy
Countsil, etc.

CRICKLUM | Course of study at a yune versty, *q.v.*

CUNGRADYALADE

To tell someone that one is pleased with his or her achievement. As in: 'Leamie be tha firce ta cungradyalade ya.'

CUNSERVE TUVS

A plitti cull pardy. *See* Paul Ticks.

DEAF SIT

What a nation ends up with when it spends what it hasn't got. Every Canajan guv munt, if it is to survive, needs something to wrestle to the ground. For years and years the Lib Rulls stayed in power by promising to wrestle inflation to the ground. Only when the country itself was flat on its back did the Lib Rulls declare victory, and promptly lost the next election because they had nothing left to wrestle to the ground. Elected in their place, the Cunserve Tuvs set out to wrestle the constooshn to the ground, a process largely derailed by then Premier Clyde Wells of Noophun Lund, remembered as the man who put the stink in distinct society. The Lib Rulls then regained power at the next election by promising to wrestle the deaf sit to the ground. Such is the pattern of freestyle wrestling as practised by Canajan paul titians.

DEE FENCE OF

Carried on for the purpose of resisting attack. As in: 'Wimpaig played a dee fence of game throut the firce quarder.' The opposite term is off fence of, as in: 'But Kail Gree played a grade off fence of game.'

DEETROYIT

Rhymes with 'destroy it.' Large Mare Can siddy lying across the Deetroyit River from Windsor, Untario. Other Mare Can places known to Canajans are Buff Low, Tcha Coggo, and Ore Gone.

DEJA VOUS	You again?
DETERIADE	To grow worse, to be reduced in quality or ability. As in: 'Stoo bad howeez deteriaded ladely.'
DIE JEST OF TRACK	The place inside people, animals, etc., where things turn into other things.
DIRDY	In an unclean state or condition; bad (of weather); obscene (of pictures).
DISBURSE	To break up or scatter. As in: 'The demonstraders were soon disbursed by the per vinshulls.'
DISGOVER	To find. As in: 'Car Chay dizgovered the Gulfa Sen Lornz in 1534.'
DODDER	A female child.
DOOAL	Double, forming a pair. As in: Dooal wheels, dooal highway. Not to be confused with jewel, a combat between two persons.

EAU CANADA

Canada's nash null anthum justly celebrates the purity of her wadder, long the envy of the rest of the whorled, especially the You Nice States. Mare Cans have always coveted Canajan wadder, calling for a con nendal paul see under which they would share Canada's wadder on a pro rata basis. For a long time Oddawa resisted these demands, claiming that Canajans needed all their wadder for sanitary purposes. The Mare cans responded with a popular song of the period which ran:

What'll I do
When you
Have flushed
The loo,
While I
Am dry,
What'll I do?

The Mare Cans are seriously considering Canada's latest offer which is to let them have the wadder after it has been used.

EEJA	To bite fiercely, to consume. Usually with adverbial suffix 'lyve.' As in: 'Cmin quick, Susan, ur the mazkiddas (*q.v.*) ull eeja lyve!'
EFF YOU	In the event that. As in: 'Teller eff you sear.'
EGG SELLENT	Very good, of considerable merit.
EGG SEPSHUNALL	Onusual, very egg sellent.
EGGS ISLE	Long banishment from one's country.
EGG SPURT	Someone with special skill or knowledge.
EGG ZACK	Precise or accurate. As in: 'I sawer in the egg zack same place as lass time.' The adverbial form is egg zackly.

GRADE HORNED HARASS

40

EH?

Rhymes with hay. The great Canajan monosyllable and shibboleth, 'eh?', is all things to all people. Other nations may boast their interjections and interrogative expletives — such as the Mare Can 'huh?', the Briddish 'what?', the French *'hein?'* — but none of them can claim the range and scope of meaning that are encompassed by the simple Canajan 'eh?' Interrogation, assertion, surprise, bewilderment, disbelief, contempt — these are only the beginning of 'eh?' and already we have passed beyond the limitations of 'huh?', 'what?', *'hein?'*, and their pallid analogues.

To begin with, 'eh?' is an indicator, sure and infallible, that one is in the presence of an authentic Canajan speaker. Although 'eh?' may be met with in Briddish and Mare Can litter choor, no one else in the world 'eh?s' his way through life as a Canajan does, nor half so comfortably. By contrast, 'huh?' is a grunt; 'what?' foppish and affected; and *''hein?'* nasal and querulous. Whereas 'eh?' takes you instantly into the speaker's confidence. Only 'eh?' is frank and open, easy and unaffected, friendly and even intimate.

Viewed syntactically, 'eh?' may appear solo or as part of a set of words, in which case it may occupy either terminal, medial, or initial position. We shall consider these briefly.

Its commonest solo use is as a simple interrogative

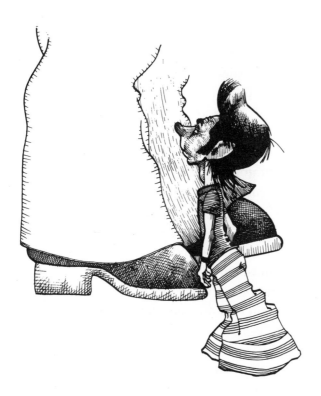

calling for the repetition of something either not heard because inaudible or, if heard, then not clearly understood. In this context 'eh?' equals 'What did you say?', 'How's that?', or in Canajan, 'Wadja say?', 'Howzat?'

According to intonation, the meaning of solo 'eh?' may vary all the way from inquiry (as we have seen) through doubt to incredulity. Here are a few examples:

'I'm giving up smoking.' 'Eh?' (A cross between what? and oh yeah?)

'Could you loan me two bucks?' 'Eh?' (Are you kidding?)

'Here's the two bucks I owe you.' 'Eh?' (I don't believe this!)

'Eh?' in terminal position offers a running commentary on the speaker's narrative, not unlike vocal footnotes:

'I'm walking down the street, eh?' (Like this, see?)

'I'd hadda few beers en I was feeling priddy good, eh? (You know how it is.)

'Well all of a sudden I saw this big guy, eh?' (Ya see.)

'He musta weighed all of 220 pounds, eh?' (Believe me.)

'I could see him from a long ways off en he was a real big guy, eh?' (I'm not fooling.)

'I'm minding my own business, eh?' (You can bet I was.)

'But this guy was taking up the whole sidewalk, eh?' (Like I mean he really was.)

'So when he came up to me I jess stepped into the gudder, eh?' (I'm not crazy, ya know.)

'En he went on by, eh?' (Just like that.)

'I gave up, eh?' (What else could I do?)

'Whattud *you* a done, eh?' (I'd like to know since you're so smart.)

'Eh?' in medial position is less common and so more prized by collectors:

'We're driving to Miami, eh?, for our holidays.' (Like where else?)

'There aren't many people, eh?, that can find their way around Oddawa like he can.' (You know as well as I do.)

'Eh?' rarely appears in initial position. Thus, while one might ask: '*N'est-ce pas qu'il a de la chance?*', Canajans could only say: 'He's lucky, eh?'

Forners are warned to observe extreme caution with 'eh?' since nothing will give them away more quickly than its indiscriminate use. Like the pronunciation of Skatchwan (only much more so), it is a badge of Canajanism which requires half a lifetime to learn to use with the proper panache.

A teacher at Arm See suggested some years ago that

'eh?' is not Canajan since it may also be found in the Knighted States, the You Kay, and Sow Thafrica. In the same way sign tists have tried to prove that hockey was not invented in Canada, but Canajans remain unconvinced, eh?

ELSIE B.O.	A collateral descendant of Dora, the scourge of Britain during World I, Elsie runs the Liquor Control Board of Untario in such a way as to make drinking within that province as difficult and unpleasant as possible. As a result, she is held in high disfavour by all serious drinkers and remembered by them with a curse in their libations. Some of her sisters plying their trade in other provinces are Elsie Beesee in Brish Clumbya and Elsie See 'em in Mantoba. A brother, Elby Ess, does the job in Skatchwan.
EMMINTIN	Cabbidal siddy of Albirda.
EM PEE	A member of the Housa Comms, *q.v.*
EM PEEPEE	A member of the per vinshull legislature.
EN	The finish or conclusion of something. As in: En produck. *Cf.* the reduplicated form 'enna,' as in: 'Looks like the enna tha lion.'

ENAY CHELL | The Nash Null (i.e. Mare Can) Hockey League, whose teams are basically Canajan players in voluntary servitude to Mare Can clubs. Compare multinational corporations, which are basically Canajan industries in voluntary servitude to Mare Can corporations, and international unions, which are basically Canajan workers in voluntary servitude to Mare Can unions.

END | The commonest conjunction in Canajan. As in: 'On the Parkway south it's stop end go."' Sometimes reduced still further. As in: 'En then I sedter . . .'

ENDY PEE | *See* Nude Democrats.

EN YOU | Canajan response to 'Have a good day.'

EUBIE SEA | Yune versty of Brish Clumbya. *Cf.* You've Tea.

EUCHRE ANIAN | An imm grunt from You Crane. Many Euchre Anians originally settled on the prayer ease where their descendants now consider themselves to be one of the found-in races, *q.v.*

EVER | An intensive widely employed in Canajan. Quite unrelated to English adverbial usage, the interrogative or inverted form is usual. 'Is it ever hot!' (It sure is hot!)

45

'Didja hava good time at the pardy lass night?' 'Did we ever!' (We certainly did!) 'Coodja gofer somepm cold?' 'Could I ever!' (You bet I could!)

EYE DENTY

The condition or character of what a thing or person is. As in the phrase Canajan eye denty, the search for which (next to hockey-watching) constitutes the nash null sport of all native sons. Native daughters have better things to do with their time.

FAIL YOURS

Elsewhere in the text we have recounted the saga of Canajan he rows. At this point frankness compels us to tell of two nash null fail yours, both of whom blew it in the same year.

The year 1837 was a very bad time for rebellions. First Lower Canada rebelled under Looie-Joe Pappy No who was born at Mun Treal like his pappy before him. In Upper Canada the rebel leader was William Lyin Mackenzie, a forner from Dundee, Scotland.

The causes of both rebellions were the same only different. But basically it was a matter of outs against ins, with the ins staying in and the outs ending up farther out.

In Upper Canada the famly was still very compact in those days, and when Mackenzie tried to loosen the ties a bit they threw him and his type into Tronna Bay. After Mac had dried himself off he went right on demanding reform and so was considered unbalanced. When reform failed to arrive Mac started a fight in a tavern but took off after the first shot. The militia chased him all the way to Nagra Falls, *q.v.*, where he thumbed his nose at them from an island in the middle of the river.

Mac moved on to the Knighted States, then as now a favourite refuge for Canajans (*See* Mare Canzation). There he conspired for a while with some Irishmen, the forerunners of the Feeny Anns (*See* Troop Ate Rot

Love-In). Eventually he came back to Canada where he hacked out a living as a writer, then as now the last resort of failed Canajans. It wasn't until very much later when his grandson, William Lyin Mackenzie King, took over Canada that Mac got even.

But while things were looking up in Upper Canada they kept going down all the time in Lower Canada.

Long discouraged with the plitti cull situation there, Pappy No believed that the creation of an Upper House in Lower Canada would put the province on an equal footing with Upper Canada. When they pointed out to him that there was no Upper House in Upper Canada but only a Lower House as in Lower Canada, Pappy No resigned in confusion from the Executive Countsil and started his own rebellion of 1837.

At first Mac offered to help Pappy, but the offer was sensibly declined on the theory that two losers don't make a winner and Pappy No was already in enough trouble by himself without Mac's assistance. In fact, he quickly followed Mac's example by heading for the Mare Can border before the real fighting started. After a decent interval all was forgiven and Pappy came back but things were never the same again. Nobody remembered him, and in old age he founded the Seniory Club at Montebello on the Oddawa River and died. His revenge on hiss tree was almost as good as Mackenzie's since he too left a grandson, Henri Bourassa, who did much to put modern Kwee Beck in the shape it's in today.

The Troubles of 1837 are always referred to as a rebellion rather than a revolution because the Canajans, while undeniably rebellious, were not revolting like the Mare Cans in 1776.

FAMLY ROOM	Part of home used for leisure or social activities such as TV watching. Formerly known as the Wreck Room when the kids were younger.
FEBBOO WARY	The month following Jannery.
FEDDER LISTS	*See* Sepper Tists.
FED RULL	Of or relating to the central guv munt of Canada. The opposite to per vinshull.
FERAL	The fed rull (*q.v.*) system in its more savage and blood-thirsty aspect. As in: 'The feral guv munt just tightened everybody's belt another notch.'
FEUDAL	Vain or useless. As in: 'Leavim lone, Linda. It's feudal targue withim, I tellya.'
FIDA	Term introducing protasis. As in: 'Fida knew weed be short, Gary, Ida took the both of them.'
FILLUM	Thin layer of very hard water found on the surface of Canajan lakes, etc., in early winner. As in: 'A fillum avice covered the pond.' A fillum is also the long roll of stuff used to take pick shirs with. As in: 'Yagoddinny colour fillum?'

FILLY	A slice off something without the bones. As in: 'Filly of soul.'
FINCH	To complete or reach the end of a given task. As in: 'Hancha finched yer litter choor sigment yet, Linda?'
FINEY	In the end; eventually. As in: 'Well, when we finey god there everyoned gaw nome.'
FIRCE	Ahead of others in time, rank, or importance. Rhymes with 'curse.' As in: 'The lass shall be firce.'
FISHLE	Duly authorized. As in: English and French are the fishle languages of Canada. Also, a person employed in a public capacity: 'According to an undenfied fishle . . .'
FITH	Next after the fourth. As in:'He took the Fith Amenment.'
FORNER	A non-Canajan. The adjective is forn.
FORCE	Large collection of trees. As in: the Canajan force industry.
FOUND-IN RACES	In keeping with the binary struck shir of Canajan paul ticks (*see* Nash Null Yewnty) there are two found-in races

in Canada although not everyone is in agreement about which two. The Bye-and-Bye Commission proceeded on the assumption that Canada was a partnership between the two found-in races of English and French, although it is beyond dispute that the In You Wit and Injuns were found-in much earlier. While it is true that there was never a partnership between In You Wit and Injuns, we have little evidence that the English and French got along any better. The claims of other groups to the title of found-in races are examined elsewhere (*see* Euchre Anians *and* Loy Lists).

FRAY TRATES

Consonant with the binary nature of Canajan plitti cull life which has been noted elsewhere (*See* Nash Null Yewnty), the guv munt helped unite the various regions of Canada by encouraging construction of a network of transcontinental railway lines. At the same time it kept them apart by a complicated system of fray trates which no one understood. This ensured a state of maximum confusion and dissension while preserving a minimum of efficiency and economy.

As one example of the problems involved, by an agreement reached in 1897 all grain shipments from the prayer ease, *q.v.*, were required, whatever their destination, to move westward through the Croze Nest Pass at very low fray trates. It was soon realized, however, that this would cause much hardship to the Merry Times, *q.v.*, since grain consigned there would have to be trans-shipped by boat from Vancouver to Halifax via the Panama Canal. Opposition critics were quick to point out that the Panama Canal had not yet been dug, which rendered the whole operation not merely uneconomical but almost impossible.

To resolve this impasse recourse was had to a legal fiction. For many years thereafter operators only pretended to ship eastbound grain to the west coast. It was instead sent at the lower Croze Nest Pass fray trates through Four Twilliam (now the Lay Ked) during the night, thereby bringing the railroads to the verge of bankrupture or financial hernia.

Only the discovery that wheat was more important than people saved the day, although the Grand Trunk Railway had already packed it in by then. Fray trates were boosted, while passenger traffic was cleverly discouraged by exchanging freight and passenger cars wherever possible. In no time the railroads were rolling again and the passengers were flying.

FREE DUMB Our way of doing things. Opposite of Comma Nizzum.

FREET RAID What happens when an elephant engages in commercial intercourse with a mouse? Mercantile rape.

53

Freet Raid has been a Canajan death wish since 1911 when Laurier was cut down over it. Most Cunserve Tuvs believe that opening the door wide enough to turn 25,000,000 Canajans loose in the You Nice States while letting 250,000,000 Mare Cans run barefoot through the Canajan economy would be a Good Thing for us.

The Nude Democrats say Freet Raid is nothing but a free fox in a free henroost. The Lib Rull approach is more states manlike: 'Freet Raid if necessary, but not necessarily Freet Raid.' The Conserv Tuvs said: 'Freet Raid is good for you. We're going to bring it in and you'll like it.' And they did. And Canajans didn't.

FRINTSTUNTS	For example.
FUCHSIAD	On the condition or supposition that. As in: 'Fuchsiad seer asterta phone me.'

FUDDLE DUDDLE

Plitti cull put-down. The phrase caused both consternation and mystification when it first appeared in *Hansard*. The House Ways and Means Committee, after searching in vain for ways to find out what fuddle duddle means, consulted sign tists at You've Tea. They ran the phrase through the computer in the language lab and came back with this print-out: '"Fuddle" is paradigmatic of a continuum of dismissives, such as "fiddle" or "fudge." The hostile element is partly discharged or at least dichotomized by addition of the replicative suffix "duddle" on the analogy of "fiddle faddle," thereby producing the synergistic "fuddle duddle."'

This explanation satisfied nobody, least of all members of Her Majesty's Loyal Opposition who were still seething, but by that time fuddle duddle had passed forever into Canajan folklore and could not be dislodged, even by a joint address of both Houses.

FUNNAMENNUL

Basic fact or principle. As in: 'The funnamennul things apply . . .'

FURN CHUR

Movable articles in a room, such as tables, chairs, etc.

FYE ERR

A conflagration. As in: 'There wuz a three-larm fye err on Bal Oil Street lass night.'

G

GAEA'S TEA | A bitter drink first brewed by Brian Mulroney, which Jean Chrétien has been compelled to swallow. Gaea (pronounced JEE-a), also known as Gaea Tellus, was the great Earth Goddess and mother of us all, so it is fitting that the Cunserve Tuvs invoked her name when they imposed the mother of all taxes on everything Canajans buy from applesauce to zithers.

GERM KNEE | Your Peen country.

GLADDA SEEYA | *See* Harya.

GNOME	To be acquainted with someone. As in: 'J'gnome a tall?' 'Nah, bud I sauce pitcher on tha nooze.'
GODDA	*See* Hadda.
GODDEN	Perfect participle of 'to get.' As in: 'It's godden very you mid in here allva sun.'
GRADE	A number of meanings may be distinguished. Famous, as in: 'Jock Car Chay was a grade explorer.' Very good, first rate, as in: 'I feel grade.' Very well, as in: 'Things are goin grade.' There is also an ironical sense, as in: 'I think it's starna rain.' 'Oh grade!'
GRADE BRIDDEN	England, Scotland, and Wales. *See* Briddi Shyles.
GRADE EEL	Very much, considerably. As in: 'She feels a grade eel bedder thi smorning.'

GRADE LAKES

The name applied to Lakes Spearyer, Urine, Mishgan, Eerie, and Untario. Together they form the largest body of polluted fresh water in the world. The Grade Lakes are part of the Undefended Front Ear, *q.v.*, and when they were being divided up between Canada and the Knighted States the Mare Cans got more their fair share

of four of the lakes and all of Lake Mishgan. This was done long before Confed Rayshun when Bridden did Canada's bargaining for her. As usual Bridden ended up by giving the lion's share to the Mare Cans, her older and stronger offspring. This is why she was called the Mother Country.

GRADGE | A building for storing or repairing automobiles.

GRADJIT | Someone who has successfully completed school. As in: 'Sheez a gradjit of Eubie Sea.' The verbal form is 'gradjade.'

GRAKE UP | Trophy awarded annually for pre-eminence among Canajan professional football teams. The championship game itself, largely conducted by Mare Can players, has been supplanted in importance since the advent of TV by the organized bragging and drinking which accompany it.

When a telephone survey was done on the Seabee See's program 'Cross-Canada Chuck-up' everyone agreed that the football moguls fumbled badly when they expanded the league to include a bunch of Mare Can teams. Somehow Westren fans never managed to work up the same degree of hate for the Dalla Scowboys as they had for the bums from Tirana. And when Baltimore made off with the Grake Up one year Canajans were left with nothing to drink to but their memories.

GRODGE | *See* Gradge.

GUNK CONTROL | For some time now the Fedrull Minster of Just-as has been trying to find a way to control the proliferation of gunk in Canada. This is not easy since accorn to the constooshn gunk falls within pervinshull jurisdiction, and Preston Manning sez that the Feds had better keep their hans off of it. The fact remains that Canada has always produced far more gunk than she can consume and is fast running out of places to put it (*See* Lanfil Sight).

At first the Feds tried shipping Western gunk eastward and Eastern gunk westward by rail through the Croze Nest Pass, which at least kept the stuff moving and utilized a lot of empty freight cars. For a time the problem seemed to be licked, but when the Feds abolished the Croze Nest Pass fray trates (*q.v.*), Canajan gunk dealers found themselves priced out of the market and unable to compete with a flood of cheap imported gunk from Taiwan. Like so many other things lately, it marked the end of an era.

GUV MUNT | *See* Paul Ticks.

HADDA

To be obliged to do something. Cognate with Godda. As in: 'I jiss hadd tellum, Susan, I jiss hadda.' 'Well, thass life, Linda, if ya godda ya godda.'

HAIRY

Man's name. As in: 'I'm jiss wilda bout Hairy.'

HALF ACID RAIN

Although this environmental problem has long taxed both of the best Canajan brains, a solution remains elusive.

Acid rain was first discovered by a Russian sign tist, Vladimir Alexeevich Plyushin, while washing out the bed of Lake Baikal. In a paper delivered before the Soviet Academy of Science in 1947, he announced that acid rain was caused by capitalist adventurism aided by its running dogs and lackeys seeking hegemony. For this he received the Lenin Peace Prize and a dacha on the Black Sea.

Canajans, having no one else to blame for their acid rain, sought to lay it on the Mare Cans. However, an International Joint Commission, after surveying joints on both sides of the border for several years, concluded that Canda and the Knighted States were equally responsible. This brought hot denials from everyone concerned, and at last report each country was still waiting for the other to clean up its half of the act first.

HAN CHA   Interrogative phrase used to ascertain the availability of something. As in: 'Han cha goddiny matches, Rick?'

HAPPIS   *See* Quorpus.

HARYA   Like most aspects of Canajan, the salutations upon meeting or parting are highly formalized and call for precise observance.

Set orders of salutation are, of course, established in every language from French to Tagalog by inveterate custom and may not be altered or departed from without risk of the speaker's being thought an ignorant boor or, what is worse, a forner. Thus, when he is introduced to someone it is mandatory for a Frenchman of the better class to say: *'Enchanté de faire votre connaissance'* and, upon parting, *Enchanté d'avoir fait votre connaissance'.* These forms are prescribed by the venerable Académie Française and the trick of dominating the encounter (or departure) is to get in first with the phrase, thereby leaving your vis-à-vis nothing more impressive to say than a rather lame *'Enchanté, Monsieur'* (or *'Madame,'* as the case may be).

A comparable punctilio attaches to Canajan salutational usage. The invariable salutation upon meeting is 'Harya t'day?' whether the object of the remark is an old friend or someone you have just been introduced to for the first time.

Although the phrase clearly contains an enquiry as to the health of the person addressed, authorities are divided about whether the response should disclose the requested or, indeed, any information. If in doubt, the periphrastic phrase 'Priddy good,' *q.v.*, may safely be employed or, if more warmth is indicated, 'Fine thankya' is a not unidiomatic reply. But it is perfectly correct to confine oneself to a repetition of the original greeting.

If the opening remark be considered as a gambit, the collocutor may accept by replying 'Howya bin?', thereby restoring the balance of conversational power. If the gambit is to be declined, the relatively neutral phrase 'Gladda seeya' will permit the parties to proceed to the next or substantive phase of the encounter.

Because of limitations of space any discussion of the middle game is here omitted, but some aspects will be dealt with at other places in the text.

Parting rituals are similarly stylized. Among old friends 'Slong' is quite appropriate, although perhaps less satisfactory at the end of a first meeting. In the latter situation 'Seeya gen' (the 'g' is hard) is a little more cordial than 'Nice senior' which does not explicitly look forward to a renewal of the acquaintanceship. A still lesser degree of cordiality may be expressed by 'Take air,' *q.v.* The closing salutation 'Bynow' is telephonese and to avoided in conversation.

HEEDER	Warming device for ameliorating the rigours of Canajan winners.
HINGON	To hold the (telephone) line. Rhymes with 'Sing on.' As in: 'Sorry but heez tye dup. Woodja like ta hingon fur a mint?'
HIRE EYES	Multi-storied apartment or office building.
HISS TREE	Study of past events.
HOLLOW EEN	The eve of All Saints' Day. A porfesser from You've Eh? has suggested that the name may derive from the custom of hollowing out pumpkins that is associated with the festival.
HOPE FLEA	Sentence adverb much favoured by Canajans who have trouble distinguishing between etymology and entymology.
HOUSA COMMS	The lective branch of parl meant. *See* Paul Ticks.
HOWYA BIN	*See* Harya.
HUGH ESS	The Mare Can nation. *See* Knighted States. So convenient has the Hugh Ess been to the development of

the Canajan ethos that if the Hugh Ess did not exist it would be necessary to invent it. By the same token, if the Hugh Ess did not exist neither would Canada, much as in physics a magnetic north pole needs a south pole. For this reason, Canada's finest hours have always been dee fence of, witness The Whore of 1812, Confed Rayshun, etc. These and related topics are discussed elsewhere in the text. It may here be noted that the best, perhaps the only, generally accepted definition of Canajan is *Not Mare Can.*

HURCHA	Inflict harm or pain. As in: 'Jeez, Gary, diddie hurcha?' Do not confuse with Hurja, *q.v.*
HURDLE	To move with great speed. As in: 'Come to the Seeya Knee (*q.v.*) and watch the Sky Divers hurdle through the yair.'
HURJA	To perceive aurally. As in: 'Awrite, awrite, I hurja the firce time!'

I

IDA | *See* Fida.

IDDLY | Your Peen country. Rhymes with 'tiddly.' Along with Bridden, Germ Knee, Porch Gull, etc., the source of many post-war imm grunts.

IMM GRUNT | One who comes into the country as a seddler. The name is believed by some to derive from the fact that for years all heavy or unattractive work was reserved for imm grunts. Many people objected to their admission on the ground that they took jobs away from Canajans. When it was pointed out that imm grunts mostly did work which Canajans were unwilling to do, this restriction was quietly relaxed and imm grunts began to do other kinds of work as well. The name has, however, remained.

INFA STRUCK SHIR	*See* Struck Shirley.
INN TREST	Concern or curiosity. As in: 'He showed no inn trest a tall.'
INNY	Some. As in: 'The lass buses gone, Gary. Izzer inny chansova lift?'
INTA RESTING	Arousing curiosity or attention.
IN TERM	Provisional, temporary. As in: 'Sony an in term slue shun.'

JA

Second person pronoun, singular or plural. As in: didja, woodja, coodja, hadja, wyja. Often occurs in elliptical phrasal usage: 'Wineja cmover tnite, Linda?' 'Wearja go Chewsdy?' 'Hooja (properly *hoomja*) asta go?' When 'ja' follows after certain consonants (for example 'r') the variant form 'ya' may be substituted. As in: 'Hoorya goint the dance with?'

JAMEENYA

Interrogative, usually expressive or surprise of mild disbelief. As in: 'Jameenya reely sawm wither?'

JENNY

For the most part. As in: 'We're specktin jenny fine weather tday.' 'Jenny speaking.'

JERREL

Not specialized or particular. As in: 'Yget the jerrel print spill, eh?'

JEWEL

See Dooal.

JOCK TALK

The language of athaletic supporters. Once upon a time all that a fan needed to know in order to follow Canajan sporting events was the phrase: 'He shoots! He sco-o-o-res!' But those simpler days have gone forever, and while our sportscasters for the most part still lack the intellectual reach of a Howard Cosell they are running hard to catch up. To assist them, some of our community colleges have begun to offer courses in jock talk, curtailing classroom time previously allotted to majors like cosmetology in order to accommodate this newer discipline. For specific examples of jock talk *see* Beat Out, Broodle, Dee Fence Of, Ketch, Off Fence Of, Senner, and Stink Up.

This emphasis on the purely verbal aspects of sporting events is a far cry from earlier attitudes when fans went to games simply to see the opposing team's blood flow. While, in hockey at least, some emphasis is still placed on more traditional modes of play such as charging, kneeing and elbowing, spearing, butt-ending, tripping, hooking, slashing, clipping, kicking, and stick throwing, more and more attention is being paid to trading, contract negotiations, and jock talk, and the future of the game would seem to lie in those dimensions.

JOGGA FEE Study of the earth's features, population, climb it, etc.

JUNO General enquiry as to someone's knowledge or information. As in: 'Juno wear schwent?'

K

KABIT, JOHN

Canajans have never been able to make up their minds how to pronounce the name of the man who discovered Canada, or even what part he discovered. There are some who prefer the New England Kabit, as in 'habit' or 'rabbit'; others call him Kabow, to rhyme with 'Joe Blow'; or Kabott to rhyme with 'why not.'

Whatever his name, Kabit (or Kabow or Kabott) came from Iddly, by way of Bridden, which was not Grade in those days. He was thus a double forner and well qualified to become a Canajan nash null he row. He was not, of course, the first imm grunt since he made a round trip. The title of first seddler is usually reserved for Looie Hey Bear, also a forner (French) who built a farm at Sault-au-Matelot, so called because he jumped ship there in 1623.

Kabit's discovery of Canada in 1497 was nothing short of sheer genius (as he told his wife) or possibly blind luck (as it appears to us). While almost everyone else in the fifteenth century who wanted to get to the East was doing the obvious thing and sailing eastward, except for Clumbus (another Eyetalian), Kabit for some reason decided to go west. By so doing he tripped over Canada which was in the way.

No one is sure where Kabit landed, but wherever it was he took possession in the name of the King of England who later gave him ten pounds for his trouble.

Since Canada has an area of roughly 3,500,000 square miles (not counting water), this was a much better buy than Manhattan Island for which the Dutch rather foolishly paid twenty-five dollars some 129 years later. In fairness it should be said that real estate values had been going up in the meantime because of inflation, but the fact remains that, as usual, the Briddish made the better deal.

The exact location of Kabit's landfall is still a matter of much dispute among sign tists and jogga firs. All are agreed that he landed on the coast of Noophun Lund, except for some who think that it was Cape Breddon, or maybe even Labberdor.

Where he landed is, however, less important for us than the fact that he did so at all since it enabled the Briddish, for a ten-pound payment, to get ahead of everybody else as the original found-in race. The French, for example, weren't found-in until 1534 (by Jock Car Chay). We now know, of course, that the Injuns and In You Wit had been found-in much earlier, but Kabit didn't see them when he landed so they couldn't prove that they were there ahead of him. Also, since they had not paid any money, as the Briddish were always careful to do, they were considered squatters and could be safely disregarded.

KAIL GREE	The principal siddy of suthren Albirda and sight of the 1988 Winner Limpics, *q.v.*
KAM	Serene, quiet, or tranquil. The verbal form is common. As in: 'Kam down, now!'
KENDA	*See* Canda.
KENTCHA	*See* Kenya.
KENYA	Are you able to? As in: 'Kenya stop whatcher doon en gimmier hand?' The negative form is Kentcha.
KERN	Belonging to the present time, as in: kern events. The adverb is kernly.
KERRY	To convey or transport. As in: 'Kerry me back to Old Moosejaw.'
KERUL	Girl's name. As in: 'Swoff Bobbin Kerul went, hend in hend.' *Cf.* Keruline.
KETCH	To intercept the motion of. As in: 'Lindros at cenner ice ketches the shot en . . .'
KEWPIE PEE	The Kwee Beck per vinshull pleece. Later changed to

Sortie Nash Null by the Sepper Tists to show that the province is on the way out.

KIDDY   A young cat. As in: 'Whatza madder Rick?' 'I can't find the kiddy-lidder, Susan. Whereja puddit?'

KLOMIDDER   A thousand meders. One of the basic terms of Metrickery, *q.v.*

KNIGHTED STATES   The Mare Can nation. *See* Hugh Ess.

KWEE BECK   Canajan province and siddy. Stress falls on the second word. Rarely, Kuh Beck. Just as the simplest definition of Canajan is *Not Mare Can*, so the most convenient way to define Kwee Beck is *Not Anglo* (*Le Québec n'est pas une province comme les autres*). Such is the power of the Canajan negative. There is no Canajan positive.

KWEE BECKER   A French-speaking inhabitant of Kwee Beck. For English-speaking Kwee Beckers *see* Anglo.

L

LANDIG PROVINCES The Merry Times, *q.v.*, plus Noophun Lund and Labberdor.

LA SCHOOL Place where young Canajans are taught to act like lawyers. As in:

 'I done priddy good on thell sats, so I'm goyna la school necks Fall.'
 'Grade! Wareya goyn, Oddawa?'
 'Nah, Westren.'

LANFIL SIGHT The town dump.

LASS *See* Firce.

LAWN DISTENS Canajans have been infatuated with the telephone ever since Alexander Graham Bell invented the busy signal in 1874 at Brantford, Untario. That was considered a major breakthrough, since Bell didn't get around to inventing the telephone itself until 1876, and Canajans

have been calling lawn distens like crazy ever since. Their addiction to the instrument has turned the country into a nation of anglophones, francophones, allophones, and car phones.

LAWN ORDER   Canajans don't care what their neighbours are up to so long as the grass is cut. That is why any paul titian who promises lawn order is sure to get elected.

LECK SHIR   An admonition or reproof. As in: 'Mom sure gameya leck shir fur doonit.'

LEER ICKS   The words of a song.

LEERSHIP   What Canajans always vote for but rarely get.

LENTH   The linear measurement of something; the distance it extends. The verbal form is lenthen. As in: 'Sgrade, Linda, butchull hafta lenthen the sleeves.'

LIBERRY   Pronounced to rhyme with 'my berry.' A learning resources center.

LIB RULLS   A plitti cull pardy. *See* Paul Ticks.

LIMPICKS

Innernational comtition held every four years that brings together the best amacher athaletes money can buy.

LITTER CHOOR

Being preoccupied with keeping warm, the early Canajans did not take to reading and writing for a long time. The appearance of the first daily newspapers in the 1830s, however, marked a turning point. Now for the first time people had something to wrap the garbage in.

From there it was but a hop, skip, and stumble to CanLit. Those who held that Canajans were only interested in beer and hockey had to eat (and drink) their words. As McLoon may have said: 'Your Canajan is but a slob, the weakest in nature, but he is a thinking slob.' When recently the average income of Canajan writers grew to almost $3,723.57 a year (seasonally adjusted) it was apparent to even the dullest observer that Canda had become a force to be reckoned with in world litter choor.

The fact that they could never earn a living kept Canajan writers from selling out. In that way personal and national integrity were preserved. It was the Canajan way. Although a lot of quite good stuff got written, the majority of readers brought up on Hollywood and Hugh Ess network shows continued to prefer Mare Can bestsellers. Since publishers proved only too willing to oblige, the flowering of Canajan letters turned out to be a branch plant.

LOOMANUMB

Shiny stuff used for making pots and pans. *See* Bog site.

LORA C. CORD

Like most Canajan pay trots and/or nash null he rows, Lora C. Cord was a forner, an attribute which she shared with Sir John, Eh? (a Scotsman), Sham Plane (a Frenchman), and Genrull Wolfe (an Englishman). Of the nash null he rows who made it big, only Looie Real was native-born (a May Tea).

For Lora C. Cord was a Mare Can by birth, which explains much about her celebrated exploit. Long before our tale unfolds she had come to Canada with her parents, married a Canajan, and established herself on a farm in the Nagra Pninsla, when the Whore of 1812 broke out.

On that fateful day in June 1813 (this was actually during the Whore of 1813) Lora's aim was not, as hiss tree books relate, to tell the Canajans at Beaver Dam that the Mare Cans were coming, since the Canajans had already received this information from the Injuns. Besides, this is too obviously a reworking of the Paul Revere story to hold water. The truth of the matter is that Lora was a double agent and her real purpose was to let the Mare Cans know that Canajans knew that the Mare Cans were coming, while encouraging the Canajans to think that the Mare Cans did not know that Canajans knew that the Mare cans were coming. This was to prove a crucial point, since if the Canajans had known that the Mare Cans knew that the Canajans knew that the Mare Cans knew that the Mare Cans were coming, the Mare Can forces might well have been up Beaver Creek without a dam.

To accomplish her mission Lora first dressed her

younger brother Rip in one of her well-known starched bonnets and stationed him in the farmyard to milk the family cow. Then while everyone thought her safely at home, Lora made her way some twenty miles through the Mare Can and Canajan lines, stopping off in both camps to spread her message. So successful was this ruse that the Mare Cans almost didn't make it to Beaver Dam at all, in which event the battle of Beaver Dam would never have taken place. It is difficult to say whether this would have affected the outcome of the Whore of 1812 since to this day no one is sure what the outcome actually was.

In any case, that day's work ensured Lora C. Cord a place in the hearts of her fellow countrymen forever. As for the Mare Cans, we do not know in what way they rewarded this early CIA agent, but significantly a new wing was added to the family home at Queenston in 1814 while not long afterward three new cows and a bull were seen grazing in the back pasture. Local gossips made much of this at the time since Mr. Cord was still away in uniform, but although Lora survived until 1868 she never would tell.

LOY LISTS

Back in 1776 some Mare Can colonists made the mistake of betting on George III instead of George Washington. For backing a loser they were chased out,

many of them to Canda, where they and their descendants continued the same tradition.

After the Revolution Lord Dorchester drew up a list (whence the name) of persons who had adhered to the Brish Crown (in the Hugh Ess they were called Disloy Lists because of their Un Mare Can activities). Those of them who could afford it, paid their own way back to Grade Bridden. Those who could not were sent to Canda because it was cheaper to settle them there than ship them all the way back across the ocean.

Once in Canda the Loy Lists received substantial grants of land, thus providing one of the earliest examples of forn ownership, a theme which runs throut Canajan hiss tree.

In many places (*e.g.*, Noob Runzwig and Untario) the Loy Lists became the first English-speaking seddlers, thereby fostering the notion that the Mare Cans were one of the found-in races, *q.v.* People still believe this in some parts of the country.

The Loy Lists or their descendants were probably responsible for what used to be one of the commonest Canajan questions (although seldom heard today): 'Where did your father came from?'

MABEL SURP Concentrated juice of *acer saccharum*.

MACHOOR Adult, fully developed. As in: 'If you're twendy-one a rover you may be septed as a machoor stoodent.'

MANTOBA Canajan province forming the eastern end of the prayer ease. A land of many waters, among them Lake Wimpaig which is larger than Lake Untario. Mantoba was originally called the 'The Postage Stamp Province' because it was collected from the Injuns and May Tea by the Hudson's Bay Company and later traded to Canada over the objections of Looie Real.

MARE CAN

Of or pertaining to the Knighted States, its inhabitants or language. *See* Mare Canize.

MARE CANIZE

To take over financially or economically; to corrupt or pollute; to impair or destroy the Canajan eye denty by such means. *See* Mare Canzation for the nominal form, Mare Can for the adjectival.

The process of Mare Canizing is not confined to any one area of Canajan life. Besides extending to the classical elements of earth, air, and water, it also includes gassa noil, minerals, automobiles, trade unions, undertakers, school books and, what is relevant to our study, language.

The growing Mare Canzation of Canajan has long been the cause of much public concern, particularly in Letters to the Editor. But even the legalization by parl meant of English and French as the fishle languages of Canada has not prevented their Mare Canzation, and the same insidious process has afflicted both Canajan and Joual, the nash null languages. In most parts of the country one no longer hears these ancestral dialects spoken in their pure forms; both are now much corrupted by Mare Can, the language of the invader. One has only to recall the prevalence — indeed the universality — of Mare Canisms to realize how far the pristine simplicity and purity of Canajan has been impaired.

'Hopefully'; 'there's no way' (sometimes abbreviated to 'no way'); 'with it'; 'uptight'; 'rip-off'; 'tell it like it is'; 'you got it'; and 'ya better believe it' (partly Canajanized to 'ya bedder believe it') — these are only a few examples of the growing deteriation of Canajan. Indeed, it may be only a matter of time before both Canajan and Joual capitulate and Mare Can reigns supreme from sea to sea.

As a footnote to the Mare Canizing of Canada one may recall that the process of winning by losing is a familiar one to students of hiss tree: witness the economic ascendancy of Germ Knee over Grade Bridden since 1945. It seems clear that the Canajans' original mistake was to beat the Mare Cans in the Whore of 1812. As a result the Mare Cans have been on top ever since. Had the Canajans managed to lose they would still be receiving forn aid from Washington.

MARE CANZATION

The familiar term brane drane is used to denote the exodus (much deplored by stay-at-homes and paul tishuns) of talented Canajans — professors, writers, executives, artists, etc. — to the Knighted States. The reverse process (much deplored by stay-at-homes and paul tishuns) is called Mare Canzation.

MAXIMS

Canajans are still waiting for the Rochefoucauld who will assemble their maxims. Such as: 'With her you'd

84

need the patience of Jove,' or: 'It's been like that since time in memoriam.'

MAY PULL

A member of the genus *acer*, the arboreal symbol of Canada. In days of yore every Anglo child was familiar with the words of Alexander Muir's grand old song

The May Pull lea fa rem blum deer,
The May Pull lea fa rever....

but for some reason the tune never caught on in Kwee Beck and was gradually phased out in favour of 'Eau Canada.' *See* Nash Null Anthum.

MAZKIDDA

The nash null insect of Canada. A kind of gnat whose bite causes a prolonged itching sensation. Mazkidda-swatting contests are staged every spring at cottage-opening time. *See* Eeja.

MEAN ETHER

Exclusionary phrasal construction. As in: 'I shir wunt be goyn there ugayne.' 'Mean ether.'

MEER

Looking-glass. As in:
    Meer, Meer ontha wall
    Hooza fairst wunna vawl?

MELK

Opaque white liquid secreted by female mammals as food, especially for the young. Also used metaphorically, as in the Canajan proverb: 'Snow use cryin over spelt melk.'

MELL

Small disk given as an award for achievement. As in: 'Her mother deserves a mell fur puddin nup wither.' Not to be confused with 'meddle,' a mineral substance such as gold or silver sometimes used for the fabrication of mells.

MERRY TIMES, THE

The eastern Canajan provinces of Nove Skoshuh, Noob Runzwig, and Prinz Edwhyland. *See* Landig Provinces.

MERRY

To take a wife or husband; to be united in wedlock. As in: 'Harya, Susan, didja heretha nooz? Rick and Linda are gedding married necks Sarrday!'

METRICKERY

The imposition of an alien measurement system. For many generations Canajans had gone on quietly measuring out their lives in rods, perches, poles, chains, links, gills, and firkins. This was known as the Imperial System, docile acceptance of which by Canajans came to be looked on by advanced thinkers as a badge of colonial tutelage.

When Kwee Beck's Quiet Revolution of the 1960s

turned noisy (*see* Whore Measures Act) Oddawa saw the need to take people's minds off sepper tizzum (*q.v.*), not to mention inflation, OPEC, the Red Menace, the Yellow Peril, the Green Berets, the Purple Passage, the Brown Study, the Blue Room, and Agent Orange. Suddenly and without warning Canajans were living in a technicolour nightmare. Clearly, swift action by the feral (*q.v.*) authorities was needed.

Oddawa rose to the challenge by imposing the

metric system of measurement on an unsuspecting populace, and in no time people completely forgot all about their own troubles. In place of the old certainties Canajans now lived in a state of approximation. They knew more or less how long or high something was, approxiamately how much it weighed, about how far to the next town. They knew winter had arrived because their feet got cold. They no longer knew exactly how much anything cost.

It was a brilliant stroke. The introduction of kill-o-grams, kill-o-meters, kill-o-pascals, etc., spelled death to the old Imperial way of life. At last, and for the first time, Canajans were as helpless and confused as the rest of the world.

MEWNI SIPPUL   Of or relating to a town or siddy. As in: 'Heez spent hafiz life in mewni sippul paul ticks.'

MILD UP   One of the two basic terms of Canajan climatology. As in: 'It's going to mild up by Chewsdy.' The antithetical term is froze hard, as in: 'This morning the pond was froze hard.'

MINTS   Short divisions of time. *See* Quorpus.

MOGAZINS   First Nations footwear.

MONEY BAG GERENTEE

An undertaking by a vendor to refund purchase price if goods are unsatisfactory. As in: 'Oney Edens offer money bag gerentee.' This climaxed in a near-death experience for Edens when customers began returning more than they had purchased.

MOUNDIES, THE

See Arsey Em Pee.

MUNCE

A considerable period of time. Specifically, several of the twelve divisions of the year. As in: 'Jee, harya t'day, Linda? Haven seenya fur munce. Wearya bin?'

MUN TREAL

The largest French Canajan siddy, sidduaded on an island in the Sen Lornz River. Local usage favours the dialectal variant Mon Treal. According to the press, much rivalry is alleged to exist between Mun Treal, the Joual cabbidal of Canada, and Tronna, the Canajan cabbidal of Canada. But of late the two have been growing closer together, at least in appearance, due to the influence of the Knighted States, the cabbidal cabbidal of Canada.

MYNAH

Reduced by the subtraction of. As in: 'Whassa temchur?' 'Mynah sate.'

NAGRA FALLS

Famous cadaract located on the Nagra Pninsla, a strip of land lying between Lakes Untario and Eerie. Although the Canajans discovered Nagra Falls first, the Mare Cans tried to take them away during the Troubles of 1812. However, the Canajans took them back with the help of Lora C. Cord, *q.v.*, after whom the Canajan or Whore Shoo Falls were named in recognition of her services. Then they gave the smaller ones to the Mare Cans as a consolation prize for losing the war. The Canajan Falls are wider and wetter; however, under the guise of remedial work, done mostly at night with wet-back labour, the Mare Cans are believed to have built up their falls some five feet higher than Canajan ones.

NASH NULL ANTHUM

Just as Canajans have been much discombobulated in their quest for an eye denty, so they have been more than a little confused in their choice of a Nash Null Anthum. Over a period of time the process of natural selection had pretty well reduced the possibilities to three in all: 'Eau Canada', 'The May Pull Lea Fa Rever', and 'Gossafe Thick Wean', but for a long time theatre audiences were unsure about which one they should stand up for. The short-term problem was solved by remaining seated for all three, but the long-term problem remained.

At this point the guv munt intervened and set up a

Parl Meantry Committee to search out and recommend a nash null anthum for Canada. Mindful of the old saying that a camel is a horse designed by a committee, the members wisely did not attempt to write a wholly new anthum. Instead, after much deliberation they decided on 'Eau Canada' for a number of compelling reasons:

(1)   It had already been written.
(2)   A majority of Canajans almost knew the tune, although not the words.
(3)   The leer icks already existed in all four languages: English, French, Canajan, and Joual.

Here it should be recalled that 'Eau Canada' is an Anglo version of an old French Canajan boat song. The only verse that anyone remembers is the first, which runs somewhat as follows:*

*The joual version, which few Anglos know, begins: 'Eau Canada! Tear ruddy nosy you....'

Eau Canada! How roam a neigh tough land?
Troop ate rot love-in awl thigh suns come hand.
With glow ingots we seethe here eyes
That rue north Strachan unfree,
Ann's tendon guard, Eau Canada,
Wheeze tendon guard 'fore thee.
(Coarse)
Eau Canada, Gloria's unfree!
Wheeze tendon guard, wheeze tendon
guard 'fore thee.
Eau Canada, wheeze tendon guard 'fore thee!

The committee heard much argument to the effect
that the use of five tendon guards was redundant and
most of them should be cut. Given the nature of
partisan paul ticks, the fight was between those who
wanted to sever all ties and those who felt strongly that
the authorized version should remain intact. Still others
were of the opinion that it was a bit much to expect
30 million Canajans to learn new words when they
scarcely knew the old ones. After prolonged debate a
compromise was reached and only two tendon guards
were cut, one from the verse and one from the coarse.
The last few lines of the verse and coarse were thus
revised to read:

Frum faron why d'eau Canada
Wheeze tendon guard 'fore thee.
(*Coarse*)
God key power land Gloria's unfree!
Eau Canada, wheeze tendon guard
'fore thee.
Eau Canada, wheeze tendon
guard 'fore thee!

NASH NULL HE ROWS

Unlike the Knighted States or Grade Bridden, Canada has produced few nash null he rows. This is partly because most potential he rows have gone elsewhere to make it big (*see* Mare Canzation), and partly because of Canajans' innate modesty and reserve. That is why most Canajan he rows have been forners. For a brief survey of successful he rows *see* Troop Ate Rot Love-In. For unsuccessful ones *see* Fail Yours.

NASH NULL YEWNTY

At least as much has been written about nash null yewnty as about nash null eye denty. In fact the two concepts are virtually interchangeable. Without yewnty there would probably be no eye denty. And without eye denty no yewnty. To make matters even more complicated, it has been suggested that neither nash null yewnty nor nash null eye denty actually exists. If they did, why would one need to write so much about them?

While it is true that around fed rull lexshun time every plitti cull pardy talks of *preserving* nash null yewnty, we have to understand that they are speaking conceptually. Yewnty (like eye denty) has a totemic value which renders it essential to practical paul ticks. Canada could not survive for a single hour without them.

What, then, is nash null yewnty? It may be described in one sentence: Nash null yewnty is what every Canajan paul titian is *for*.

Where paul titians differ, however, is about how best to preserve (or achieve) nash null yewnty. This is what fed rull lexshuns are for. Without yewnty there would be no lexshuns. And without lexshuns no talk of yewnty. Such is the binary struck shir of Canajan paul ticks.

The same struck shir dictates that nash null yewnty is made up of many pairs, each part of which simultaneously attracts and repels the other. So we find East versus

West; Oddawa versus the provinces; rural versus urban; men versus women; English versus French. For our purposes only the last pair need only be considered; the principle in any case is the same for all of them.

It also follows from the binary struck shir of Canada that two quite different approaches exist to the question of maintaining (or achieving) nash null yewnty. These may be considered briefly as follows.

On the one hand the Sepper Tists believe that Canajans can only really come together in a meaningful way by dividing, and their main plitti cull grouping, the Peek You Pardy, is dedicated to this end. However, the Sepper Tist movement, appropriately, is itself divided into two groups: the Gradualists who see Sepper Tizzum as a slow, evolutionary process (long division), and the Extremists who seek instant gratification (short division).

On the other hand the Sepper Tists are opposed by the Fed Rullists or Bling Youlists who believe that yewnty can be achieved if enough Anglophones become Francophones. To accomplish this the Fed Rullists have spent millions of dollars on a crash course to make Anglo civil servants bling yule. But so far linguistic baptism by total immersion has produced limited results. Other authorities feel that the only solution lies in intermarriage or a crèche course, but this is clearly a long-term remedy. These two approaches in fact appear to be counterparts of the short division and long division paul sees of the Sepper Tists.

The basic weakness of the fed rull position is that it rests on a shaky premise: namely, that Anglophones speak English and Francophones speak French, both of them languages of civilization. While this may be the case in the rest of the world, it is not so in Canada where English and French are only the fishle (i.e., hypothetical or paper) languages. As we have seen, the nash null (i.e., actual or street) languages are Canajan and Joual, and it is highly problematical whether these, a matter of birthright, can ever become interchangeable. It is difficult enough to train an Anglophone to be a Francophone; it is almost certainly impossible to train a Canajan speaker to become a Joual speaker. Yet until we can accomplish the latter metamorphosis, any likelihood of a truly bling yule country and hence of nash null yewnty seems remote.

NICE SENIOR   *See* Harya.

NOT BAD   Canajan is unusual among highly developed languages in that it virtually dispenses with superlatives. Not for Canajans the Mare Can extremes of 'Terrific!' or 'Lousy!' or even the more modest Briddish, 'Awf'lly good' or

'Awf'lly bad.' A Canajan speaker achieves the same effect by an adroit use of meiosis: 'Jalike mnoo soot, Nancy?' 'Not bad.' 'Howdtha Leafs do lass nite, Rick?' 'Not good.'*

One must exercise great care with these and cognate forms, among which Mare Cans and imm grunts may easily lose their way. Thus 'Not bad' really means 'good'; while 'Not too bad' means 'fair,' 'so-so,' or even 'quite good.' On the other hand, 'Not good' means 'quite bad.' No distinction is made between adjectival and adverbial forms.

A Canajan speaker will rarely if ever say 'bad.' This is not because of any innate desire to avoid wounding the other person's susceptibilities but because 'bad' and for that matter 'good' are simply unidiomatic and not available under normal circumstances. Thus, if one wishes to express the sense of 'bad' one must, as we have seen, resort to periphrasis. And the same rule applies in adverbial contexts. 'Howza wife feelin, Gary?' 'Not bad' (i.e., better), or 'Not good' (i.e., poorly), or even 'Not too good' (i.e., worse).

NOT GOOD   *See* Not Bad.

*Cf. the fairly recent intrusion of Mare Can 'Great!' Canajanized as Grade! q.v.

NOWER	A division of time equivalent to sigsdy mints. As in: 'See yan bowda nower.' *See* Quorpus.
NUCULAR	Pronounced 'nuke-you-ler.' Anything involving or using nucular energy.
NUCULAR WAIST	What's left of nucular fuel after the juice has been extracted.
NUDE DEMOCRATS	Some day when Canajan society has been stripped of the excesses of cabbidalism the bare face of social justice will be exposed. Such is the aim of the Nude Democrats. Originally the party name was Si-Si-Ef, but the Si-Si sounded too Tex-Mex for Canajan consumption and the Ef word put some people off, so they changed the name to Nude Democrats to show that (a) they are democratic and (b) they have nothing to hide. No other Canajan plitti cull pardy can make these claims.

ODDAWA

The cabbidal siddy of Canada. Sidduaded at the confluence of the Oddawa, Reedough, and Gaddino rivers. The name derives from the Algonkian word *adawe* meaning 'to buy and sell.' Most plittical sign tists consider this no improvement over the previous name of the place, Buytown.

ODDUM

Between summer and winner, *q.v.*

OFF TEN

Frequently, many times.

OFFUV

Double prepositional construction. As in: 'Rick, woodja kinely takeyer feet offuv the furn chur!'

OH PEEPEE

The Untario per vinshull pleece.

ONCOMFORTABLE

Not comfortable.

ONCOMMITTED

The great Canajan stance.

ONSUCCESSFUL

Not achieving or attaining success.

ONUSUAL	Not usual.
OOT	*See* aboot.
OSHWA	Untario siddy, home of Jerrel Moders.
OUIDA	Prefix introducing a conditional construction. As in: 'Two badger cooden come lass week, Susan. Ouida loveda senior.'
OWER	*See* Nower.
OWN SOUND	Town near Jorjan Bay, Untario.

PADDIO | Outdoor living area, often paved, adjoining a house.

PAIN | The exchange of money for goods or services. As in: 'Let's gopher accuppla beers.' 'Shir, who's pain?'

PAM | Inner surface of the hand; also a kind of tropical tree. *See* Pam Sundy.

PAMERSTON | The first syllable as in 'Pam.' The town of Palmerston, Untario.

PAM SUNDY | The Sundy before Easter.

PARDY | 1. A social gathering or reception. As in: 'Hi, Linda! Weir havena pardy Sarrday. Kenya come?' 2. A plitti cull grouping. *See* Paul Ticks.

PARL MEANT | The governing body of Canda, composed of the Housa Comms, the Cent, and the Guvner Genrull. *See* Paul Ticks.

PARLEL | Things running along at the same distance from other things. As in: Parlel lions never meat; the Fordy-ninth Parlel.

PAUL SEE | A course of action, particularly in nash null affairs. As in: gassa noil paul see; forn paul see; Mare Can takeover paul see, etc.

PAUL TICKS   In Canda, the art of the impossible. The adjectival form is plitti cull. Canajan paul ticks is based on the pardy system, the main plitti cull groupings being: Lib Rull, Cunserve Tuv, Rough Form, the Block, and Endy Pee. A brief discussion of the Canajan plitti cull system is here given because of its linguistic interest.

The Chief Executive was formerly known as the Pry Minster because of a belief which prevailed at the time that the guv munt should be concerned with what went on in people's bedrooms. As a result of this widely held view, an intensive program of bedroom surveillance was carried out over a period of years by the Arsey Em Pee, *q.v.* After the lapse of much time and several Royal Commissions (including one on the Stadus of Women) it became apparent that, in fact, very little of interest actually went on in Canajan bedrooms and the whole program was quietly discontinued with the brief announcement: 'The state has no business in the bedrooms of the nation.' At the same time the Chief Executive's title was changed to Prime Inster and all-night sittings of Parl Meant were abolished with no discernible loss of efficiency.

The Canajan Parl Meant is bicameral in struck shir,

consisting of the Housa Comms or Green Chamber (for go) and the Cent or Red Chamber (for stop). Members of the Housa Comms, known as Em Pees, are elected at quinquennial fed rull lexshuns held every four years. Members of the Cent are called Centres and are appointed by the guv munt in power. The Cent was intended to be the place for 'sober second thoughts' about proposed guv munt legislation. For this reason Sir John, Eh?, *q.v.*, although a nash null he row, was never made a Centre.

Plitti cull sign tists equate the Housa Comms and the Cent to a Lower House and an upper House, although when the Parl Meant buildings were constructed in 1867 or thereabouts both chambers were sensibly located on the main floor. This was done to avoid any unfavourable comparison based on altitude, and also because elevators had not yet been invented and no one could agree on who should walk up the stairs.

This equitable arrangement, which has continued down to the present day, permits plitti cull debates and name-calling to be conducted simultaneously in both chambers at the same level, thus keeping Em Pees and Centres fully occupied while all important decisions are being made by the Cab Net, *q.v.*

PAUL TITIAN	A practitioner of paul ticks, *q.v.*
PEEANNA	Musical instrument with metal strings struck by hammers which are worked by levers from a keyboard. *See* Penis.
PEDAL	Part of the corolla of a flower. As in: 'Hey, lookit the size of the pedals on that buddercup, willya!'
PEEDERBURRA	*Also* Peerburra. Municipality in Central Untario.
PEEK YOU	A plitti cull pardy in Kwee Beck. *See* Nash Null Yewnty.
PENIS	Person who plays the peeanna.

PENTZEL	A thin cylinder of wood containing a core of graphite, used as a writing instrument before computers were invented.
PERADIZE	Heaven; state of bliss; any new resort area or housing subdivision.
PERAGRAPH	A passage in a document or book separated from what precedes it by indenting the first line.
PERALIZED	Crippled, rendered powerless.
PERRY SOUND	A town on Jorjan Bay, Untario.
PICK SHIR	A painting; a graphic impression. Often used metaphorically, as in: 'Dya wameta drawya a pick shir?'
PIDDY	Sympathy; cause for regret. As in: 'Whadda piddy!'
PINE EAR	A person who first enters or settles a region.
PLENNY	Quite, fully. As in: 'It's plenny gooda nuff fur me.'

PLITTI CULL *See* Paul Ticks.

PLITTI CULL SIGNS For many years plitti cull sign tists have been trying to figure out what makes Canajans tick. According to one theory, the clock stopped when Laurier was cut down. Others are not sure it ever got started.

Canajans have always produced more guv munt than they can consume. At every level — Fed Rull, Per Vinshull, Mewni Sippul — Canajans are over-governed from dawn to dusk. After dark the sidewalks are rolled up in most cabbidal siddies: Oddawa, Tronna, Wimpaig, Rajinah, Sane John. Next morning the whole process starts over again.

Studies by You've Tea sign tists have shown that the age-old battle of rights vs. wrongs, ups vs. downs, ins vs. outs waged by the two major parties over the years is wholly symbolic. Sir John, Eh? understood this make-believe quality, which is why he called his own grouping The Liberal-Conservative Party. Faces aside, there is little practical difference between the two adversaries, and in consequence Canajan plitti cull debate is largely a matter of going through the emotions.

Since the game is symbolic, the leader with the most powerful symbol always wins. Sir John, Eh? relied on a whisky bottle. William Lyin Mackenzie King won with a crystal ball. In later jousts a shrug vanquished lost

luggage, a rose triumphed over a banana, and blarney beat out pinchy-pinchy. So it goes. In the musical comedy of plitti cull life Canajans watch their universe unfolding to the clash of symbols.

PLOOTER Someone who causes plooshn. *See* Half Acid Rain.

POOR LEN Member of a group of French Canajans who claim that their ancestors came over on the *Grande Hermine* with Jock Car Chay. Although they would rather die than admit it, Poor Lens are in fact the mirror image of their Anglo counterparts, the Loy Lists. Both groups share an identical set of beliefs, namely, that (a) they are purer than pure; (b) anyone whose ancestors arrived in the country later than theirs did is not authentic; (c) they are the salt of the earth and all others are below the salt; and (d) no one appreciates them. Poor Lens and Loy Lists spend most of their time remembering.

PRACKLY Almost.

PRAYER EASE The western Canajan provinces of Mantoba, Skatchwan, and Albirda.

PRIDDY GOOD Not really very good. *See* Not Bad.

PRIME INSTER	*See* Paul Ticks.
PROE JUICE	Agger culcherl producks.
PROBABUILDY	Likelihood. As in: 'There's a strong probabuildy that I'll metre after the lexshir.'
PROM	Something difficult to deal with or understand. As in: 'Tha prom wither is . . .'
PROSSNT	Along with Cath Licks, one of the major religious denominations in Canda. In some provinces Prossnt children go to public schools while Cath Lick children are sent to Seppert Schools. This helps preserve the ecology.
PRY MINSTER	*See* Paul Ticks.

QUORPUS

Fifteen mints past the hour. As in: quorpus three; quorpus aid. Other time indicators are: quorda; tempus; happis; tenta. Thus: quorda sevn; tempus five; happis leven; tenta too. The period of sixty mints is capable of various divisions in Canajan. For example: fie mints; twenny mints; haffa nower; fordy mints. 'Wenl I seeya?' 'Bouta nower.' 'Wendy ryve?' 'Fore thirdy.'

R

RAPE AIRS Persons responsible for paying mewni sippul property taxes. As in: 'A delegation of rape airs appeared before Siddy countsil to oppose hire eyes plans.'

RAY JAYSHN Stuff that comes off nucular stuff. *See* Nucular.

RAY JOE Wireless telegraphy.

RECRATION Pertaining to pastime or entertainment. As in: recration airya.

REEL Very. As in: 'Mail reel early for Christmas.' Also genuine. As in: 'Izzie fa reel?'

REFERENDUMB Process of referring the same stupid question over and over again to the electorate in hopes that one day they will get sick and tired and vote yes just to stop the dentist's drill.

REVISION IZZUM

The hiss tree of Canajan paul ticks is fraught with miscalculations, the effects of which are felt long after the miscalculators have left the plitti cull stage. Two which changed the course of everyone's lives were Sir John Eh?'s decision to build a transcontinental railway when a fleet of buses would have been much cheaper, and Pierre Trudeau's decision to introduce bilingual corn flakes boxes before the ad agencies had figured out how to say 'snap, crackle, and pop' in French.

Canajan plitti cull marriages are noted for the brevity of the honeymoon, as witness the following sobering second thoughts:

Jean Chrétien: The little guy from Shawinigan is in again.

Lucien Bouchard: Canada if necessary, but not necessarily Canada.

Jean/John Charest: John-schmon, so long as you're curly.

Preston Manning: Better a redneck than a deadneck.

Alexa McDonough: Make love not politics.

RIDE

Present tense of Rode, *q.v.*

RILLYA

Untario siddy called 'Mariposa' by Stephen Leacock, one of its summer residents and an economist turned humorist who couldn't spell very well. As an economist

112

Leacock was quite humorous; as a humorist he was quite economical.

RODE   To have conveyed information, etc., by epistolary means. As in: 'I rode him a lerr boudid, Rick, buddid din dooa bidda good. He never sot.'

ROOT   A territory or round for non-urban postal delivery. As in: Rule Root, abbreviated in writing to R.R. *See* Rowt.

ROQ   The Rest of Quebec. What's left of *la belle province* after the Anglos hold their own referendumb (*q.v.*). ROQ's nash null flag: the fleur-de-lis with one lobe missing. Their nash null anthum: 'Memory.' *See* Anglodesh.

ROWT   A territory or round visited by a person making deliveries. As in: paper rowt, melk rowt, etc. *See* Root.

RULE ROOT   *See* Root.

SASTOON | A siddy on the South Skatchwan River, Sastoon started out life as a temperance colony but the seddlers soon fell off the wagon.

SCHNOOK | A big wind from the West.

SCOTT | To have, to possess. As in: 'I tellya, Susan, Walter scott a nerve iffie thinksile wait forum.'

SEE ARTY SEE | White knight and watchdog of the airwaves. The inventor, preserver, and enforcer of Canajan Content, *q.v.*

SEEYA GEN | *See* Harya.

SEEYA KNEE | The Canajan Nash Null Exa Bishun held annually at Tronna.

SEN LORNZ RIVER | One of the great rivers of the world, stretching from Lake Untario in the west to the Strait of Belial in the east. Originally discovered by Jock Car Chay who entered and circled the Gulfa Sen Lornz on his first visit in 1534 but somehow missed the entrance to the river itself. This bothered Jock so much at the time that he had to come back two years later to find out where all the water was coming from.

SENNER	The middle point; also a group of buildings or stores within a single architectural plan. As in: senner ice; the Teedee Senner in Tronna; Siddy Senner, etc.
SENTS	Sense. As in: 'I tellya, Linda, it jiss dough make sents.' Sents meaning sense should not, however, be confused in Canajan with sense meaning cents. Thus one would say: 'He made me feel like two sense.'
SEPPERT SCHOOLS	*See* Prossnt.
SEPPER TISTS	*See* Fedder Lists.

SEPPER TIZZUM	An organic disease affecting the Canajan body politic.

Both eastern and western strains have been detected. Cause: a belief that the parts are greater than the whole. Symptoms: a chip on the shoulder, itchy feet. Cure: patience, patience.

For a long time many Kwee Beckers, a.k.a. Sepper Tists, have dreamed of taking their piece of the Sen Lornz River and starting a new country outside Canada. When cooler heads pointed out that Kwee Beck's stretch of the river was connected at each end to someone else's water, the Sepper Tists reluctantly agreed to settle for a new country inside Canada. This proved a great disappointment to Newfoundland Premier Brian Tobin who had figured that if Kwee Beck left Canada it would shorten the flying time between St. John's and Oddawa by about two hours.

Sepper Tists are proud of the fact that they were the first people in the country to abandon the old Imperial system of measurement, whence their motto 'Mètres chez nous.'

SERN
An unspecified quantity of something. As in: A sern amound. The adverbial form is serny as in: 'I serny intenna teller.'

SHAM PLANE
Samuel de Sham Plane, a forner and the Father of New France, was one of the earliest Canajan nash null he

rows. Born in France, he spent many years discovering parts of Canada that no one else had been able to find.

From the time that he was a young boy Sham Plane had been very good at finding things. He didn't discover Canada, but that was only because it had already been discovered (by Jock Car Chay). But he did discover much of present-day Kwee Beck and Untario, including the Oddawa River, Jorjan Bay, and Lake Nippy Sing, which he bought from the Injuns for a song.

Occasionally Sham Plane lost things as well. One day while out discovering Jorjan Bay he slipped and fell on his astrolabe which was not found again until about 300 years later.

Sham Plane also did much for the Injuns. Up to that point they had left each other pretty much alone except for occasional hairdressing parties. But Sham formed alliances with them and so taught entire tribes to kill each other just like white people. Then he imported the first missionaries to finish the job of civilizing them.

Sham was a great colonizer. To teach the Injuns white man's ways he took their lands from them and brought in shiploads of people from France to settle there. He founded Kwee Beck Siddy and Three Rivers which, as he was unable to speak English, he called Trois Rivières. He couldn't count very well either since there is actually only one river, the St. Maurice. He encouraged agriculture, cut down trees, invented pollution, and generally put New France on the map.

118

As soon as New France amounted to something the Briddish came in and took it away from the French, thus demonstrating to the Injuns the importance of the lesson which Sham Plane had already taught them. This was in 1629 during rehearsals for the Wolfe-Mont Kam war games later on. However, the Briddish were too busy sending surplus Scotsmen to the Merry Times, *q.v.*, to bother much with New France, so they gave it back to Sham Plane a few years later. Had they not done so it would not have been necessary for Gen Rull Wolfe to take it away from the French a second time. It is upon such small points that the great events of hiss tree sometimes turn.

Sham Plane made maps, wrote books, commuted yearly between France and Canada, married a twelve-year-old girl, Hélène Boullé, and died. They named Lake Sham Plane after him. They named Saint Helen's Island near Mun Treal after Mrs. Sham Plane.

SHAWVL   A town in Pontiac County, Kwee Beck, lying northeast of Oddawa.

SHEEHAN EYE   One of several well-known recipients of confidences. As in: 'I jiss canned tellier, Susan; it's between sheehan eye.' Similarly: 'Between ewan eye.'

SHIDDY

Of inferior quality or style. As in: 'So how was the game lass night?' 'Shiddy.'

SIGN TIST

Person well-versed in a branch of signs. As in plitti cull sign tist, soshul sign tist, nucular sign tist, etc.

SINS

Prepositional or conjunctive aid signifying the passage of time. As in: 'Kail Gree's reely groan sins the lass whore.'

SIR JOHN, EH?

The Father and Mother of his country, Sir John, Eh? started out life with every quality necessary for Canajan greatness.

To begin with he was a forner, always a great boost up the ladder, witness the example of Seedy How (a Mare Can). Since Canajans are taught from their youth onward that they can produce nothing of value, it follows that anything from someplace else must be better.

Secondly, he was the very best kind of forner (i.e., a Scot), one of that indomitable breed who, totally unable to make a living at home, profitably exported bagpipes and banking to the farthest shores of Empire.

Thirdly, he was (so far as Canada is concerned) one of that most fortunate of Scots, namely a Macdonald, a family rivalled in the Canajan Hall of Fame only by the Mackenzies. One need but leaf through the pages of any hiss tree book to realize how much Canajans owe to those doughty Scottish pine ears of another age. And even to this day a boy named Mackenzie Macdonald (or possibly Macdonald Mackenzie) would clearly be destined for great things. That is, if he could ever get people to stop calling him 'Mac.'

John, Eh?'s arrival on the Canajan plitti cull scene came at a critical juncture. In those days the country consisted of Upper Canada and Lower Canada, and the two divisions were engaged in constant bickering and strife. The Upper Canajans felt that because they were upper they should always be on top, while the Lower Canajans objected to being downstream and so always on the receiving end. In an attempt to overcome this rivalry their names were changed to Canada East and Canada West, but the twain never did meet.

The brilliant thought then occurred to John, Eh? that rather than have the Eastern and Western divisions not getting along in a simple union of two, it would be better for them not to get along in a larger union of all the Brish North Mare Can colonies. So taken was he with this idea, which occurred to him one morning while shaving, that he immediately summoned the Fathers of Confed Rayshun to Charltown. There he soon convinced them that a fed rull union would be the solution to all their problems.

Some of the Fathers feared there might be conflict between the future provinces. 'Since none of us is getting along as it is,' he told them, 'we would be much farther ahead not getting along all together.'

Other Fathers said they couldn't afford it, but John, Eh? was not to be deflected from his purpose. 'Since none of us has any money,' he replied, 'let us pool our deficits and print some money. If we keep it in constant circulation in the provinces, the fed rull guv munt will never have to redeem it.'

This display of logic convinced the last doubting Father and the Canajans then petitioned the Brish Guv Munt to pass the Beanay Act which, by dividing everything up between the fed rull guv munt and the provinces, with some overlapping, left things in a state of imbalance that kept everyone on his neighbours' toes forever after.

Macdonald was knighted Sir John, Eh? by the Queen for all his troubles and proclaimed a nash null he row. He was also named Prime Inster of the new nation, a post which he occupied until the next fed rull lexshun when he was defeated at the polls. His immediate successor was named (you guessed it) Mackenzie.

SKANNA   In a manner of speaking, as it were. As in: 'Howja doontha zams?' 'Skanna harda say.'

SKATCHWAN   The middle Canajan province out on the prayer ease; the grainery of the West. Very prehistoric, the parts that aren't cretaceous being quite precambrian.

SKENE   A popular winner sport. As in: 'At the Winner Limpicks Canajans placed twenny-secken in downhill skene.'

SLONG   The principal Canajan salutation on parting. *See* Harya.

SLOVAT   Motive power of the earth. Witness the Canajan proverb: 'Slovat makes tha world ground.'

SLUE SHIN	*See* In Term.
SNOTTA	An indicator of resignation. As in: 'Snotta bitta use, Rick. Shwoodent gimmier chance texplane.'
SONY	Merely, just. As in: 'Sony the firce time they binta Wimpaig.'
SOUR	Unit of time containing sigsdy mints. As in: 'That sit for thi sour.'
SPADED	Fixed.
SPEINCK	To slap on the buttocks. Rhymes with beinck, *q.v.* Oddawa Valley Canajan.
SPYDA	Notwithstanding. As in: 'I'm still goan, Susan, spyda whatcha say.'
STAIN TOUCH	What Canajns say when taking leave of a friend. Variants are 'Take Air' and 'Nice Senior.'
STINK UP	To play hockey inadequately in a given location. As in: The Leafs stunk up the Gardens lass nite. *See* Jock Talk.

STRENTH | Vigour, bodily power. The verbal form is strenthen. As in: 'The guv munt's bling yule paul see has (or hasn't) helped strenthen nash null yewnty.'

STRUCK SHIRLEY | Of or pertaining to building. As in: 'The howsiz struck shirley sound.' The nominal form is struck shir.

SUG JEST | To propose. Also occurs in the nominal form sug jest shun.

SUNDY | The first day of the week. Other Canajan days are: Mundy, Chewsdy, Wensdy (Weddens Day on the Seabee See), Thursdy, Fridy, and Sadder Day (Sarrday).

SWEDDER | Knitted woolen garment covering upper part of the body.

TAMARA | The day after today.

TARE ISTS | People who commit acts of tare ism. The ones we support are called Free Dumb Fighters.

TELECANAJAN | As befits a laconic people Canajans are the world's greatest users of the telephone. This seeming paradox may perhaps be explained by the fact that most Canajan telephone users aren't saying anything, as any innocent eavesdropper can verify. To help conceal this a mini-language has been developed which gets them through the exigencies of disembodied conversation without facial or manual aids.

Canajan telephonese, or telecanajan, bears traces of brachylogy. It is strongly marked by apheresis, litotes, and apocope, while dieresis, syneresis and, above all, stichomythia are pronounced. Here is a brief specimen:

'Low.'
'Sooin?'
'Snot home. Hooz peekin?'
'Rick. Thatchoo Linda?'
'Ya. Harya t'day?'
'Priddy good, en you?'
'Grade.'
'Whuzz dooin?'

'Nawmuch. Yagoyna tha game?'

'Ya bet. Godda cuppla graze.'

'Hooz plane?'

'Tronna en Deetroyit.'

'Hooja like, Tronna?'

'Na, eye god Deetroyit by two gowals.'

'Zarrite? Lye haver callya?'

'Ya, wenja spectre?'

'Bouta nower.'

'Asterta callme willya?'

'Sure. Seeya.'

'Bynow.'

'By.'

TEMPA CHOOR   The degree of heat or, particularly in Canda, of cold. As in: 'The present tempa choor outside our stoodios is aid degrees sell shuss.'

TEMPUS   *See* Quorpus.

TENTA   *See* Quorpus.

TENSE   A game for two or four persons who hit a ball with rackets over a low net. Also attributively, as in: Tense elbow.

TETNICKLE	Pertaining to an art, science, or trade; connected with industrial arts or applied science. As in: 'stoo tetnickle fer me,' or 'he gradjated from tetnickle school.'
THANG SLOT	Formulaic expression of gratitude.
THROUT	In every part. From C to C, geographically speaking. As in: 'Yukkin seat throut Canda.'
TICKELRY	To an exceptional degree, especially. As in: 'I'm not tickerlry interessted in scene the bally.'
TIRANA	Cabbidal siddy of Untario after Premier Mike Harris's Commonsense Revolution has turned the province into a Third World country. A.k.a. Tronna.

TOB	Opposite of boddum, *q.v.*
TOOB	*See* Choob.
TOLE	Full or complete in scope. As in: 'The tole effect.' Or: 'It's tole war out there on the Parkway.'
TOLEY	Entirely, completely. As in: 'Sheez toley withit.' Note also the substantive form 'tole' as in: 'Joe Carter had a two-game tole of four arby eyes.'
TOLEY SOLE DOUBT	Why you can't get tickets.
TORE SHIR	The infliction of severe pain. As in: 'Mnoo shoes look good, Susan, bud they're tore shir to wear.'
TORRANCE	Large quantities of water. As in: The rain came down in torrance (alternatively, in buggets).
TRONNA	*See* Tirana.
TROOP ATE ROT LOVE-IN	The quality which Canada commands in all her sons. Despite this adjuration Canada has produced few troop ate rots and even fewer nash null he rows. One such was Darsima Gee, assassinated at Oddawa in 1868 by members of an early feminist group, the Feeny Anns

or Mothers of Confed Rayshun. Others, discussed elsewhere in the text, were Looie Real, Sham Plane, Sir John, Eh?, Jock Car Chay, and Lora C. Cord.

TUDGE   To reach; to come in contact with. As in: 'He prackly tudged boddum wennie dove.'

TURBID   The *casus belli* of the Great Canada-Spain Fish War of '95.

TWENDY   Twice ten. One counts thus in Canajan: twendy (or twenny), thirdy, fordy, fifdy, sigsdy, seveny, eighdy, ninedy (or niney), a hunnerd.

UFF YOU Some, but not many. As in: 'Watch for uff you I-see patches on tha sidewalk.' Do not confuse with Eff You, *q.v.*

UNDEFENDED FRONT EAR Originally the Canajan-Mare Can boundary line. In view

of Canada's inability to Keep the Mare Cans Out, the expression is now largely meaningless and exists on the one hand as a political cliche and on the other as a reference to the invasion of Canada by Hugh Ess television.

UNTARIO The uncola province.

URINE Second largest of the Grade Lakes, *q.v.* Much polluted, whence the name.

VENNILASHIN | What you get when you vennilate a place.

WADDER LOO | Town adjoining Kitchner, Untario.

WESLEY | Directional indicator. As in: 'Yukon espect strachan wesley wins tamara.'

134

WESTREN	Opposite of eastren. As in: 'Tha Yune versty uv Westren Untario.'
WHORE	Expression of loathing or fear. As in: The whore of it! See also Macduff's outburst upon discovering King Duncan's murdered body which he (erroneously) attributes to the three witches whom he addresses in these words: O whore, whore, whore! Tongue nor heart Cannot conceive nor name thee! The adjectival form is 'whorebull.'
WHORE MEASURES ACT	For years people had been trying to clean up Canajan streets, but with scant success. As long as sin took place after dark and no one could recognize the women of the street, most civic fathers turned a blind eye while the girls turned a trick. But when the ladies of the evening began to extend their turf into the afternoon and even mid-morning, causing both industrial productivity and school attendance to decline sharply, it became clear that Something Had To Be Done. But what? As fast as local authorities passed laws against the skin trade, the Spreme Court of Canda, with its superior knowledge of the subject, struck them down.

Finally in desperation someone recalled the Whore Measures Act, a statute that had been enacted during World War I when farm boys coming to the big city to enlist needed special protection. The statute was nothing if not versatile, having been last used to cleanse Vancouver's streets after Pearl Harbor. Why not (people said) invoke it against this new peril?

Well, before you could say civil liberties they called out the Army, which knows better than anyone how to deal with camp-followers. In a twinkling every last troublemaker was off the streets and into the jug. The Department of Sanitation never had it easier and Canajan streets had never been cleaner.

WHORLED	The planet we all live on. Often used attributively, as in: 'Canajan athaletes are whorled class nowdays.'
WINCHELL	Meteorological term. As in: 'tha winchell factor.'
WINNER	The principal Canajan season, immediately preceding summer.
WIMPAIG	The cabbidal siddy of Mantoba.
WORSH	To cleanse oneself or one's clothing.

WRENCH | To worsh lightly with wadder.

Y

YAGODDINY
Interrogative to ascertain the availability of something. As in: 'Yagoddiny ornjuz? melk?' etc.

YASKT
To make all necessary enquiries; to request information. As in: 'I'm awfully glad yaskt.'

YEAR TATE
Annoy, exasperate. As in: 'Smar nup, eh? Yer beginnin ta year tate yer mother.'

YESDAY
The day preceding today.

YOMEE
Rhymes with 'show me.' Indicator of pecuniary or other obligation. As in: 'Yomee twenny sense.' Or 'Yagodda tellme, Linda. Yomeea nanser.'

YOU ESS
See Hugh Ess.

YOU KAY
See Briddi Shyles.

YOUR PEEN
Of or pertaining to the connent of Yourp. As in: 'Since Grade Bridden joined the Your Peen Yune Yin, wherezit leave the Brish Commwealth?'

YOUPIE EE EYE
Yune versty of Sharltown. Whence the college yell: 'YOUPIE EE EYE! YOUPIE EE EYE! EE EYE, EE EYE, OWE!'

YOU'VE TEA	Academy of hire learning in Tronna. *Cf.* Eubie Sea.
YUDAMEAN?	Sentence filler used to rest the speaker's brain while the tongue is still working.
YUD	Conditional statement expressing will or intention. As in: 'Untario — izzer inny place yud rather be?'
YUNE VERSTY	Instooshn of hire edge cayshn. Canda boasts many whorled class yune versties, some of which are discussed elsewhere: *see* Eubie Sea, Westren, Youpie Ee Eye, You've Eh?, You've Tea.

ZARRITE | Interrogative response to an affirmative verbal statement, often indicating mild disbelief. As in: 'Susan, Ike ud reely gopher you!' 'Zarrite?'

ZIFF | As would be the case if.

ZMARRA FACK | Introductory verbal aid. As in: 'Zmarra fack I wuz jiss goy nowt wennie rived.'